R. Eric Reidenbach
Terry C. Wilson
Gordon W. McClung
Reginald W. Goeke

The Value Driven Bank

Strategies for Total Market Satisfaction

IRWIN
Professional Publishing*
Burr Ridge, Illinois
New York, New York

BANK**L**INE™
A BankLine Publication

ISBN 1-55738-773-7

Printed in the United States of America

BB

1 2 3 4 5 6 7 8 9 0

ZGraphics, Ltd.

CONTENTS

FIGURES AND TABLES

TABLES

INTRODUCTION

As banking books go, this book is probably unlike any other book that you have read. We have intentionally crafted a book that is designed to question the way you manage your financial institution. We think you will find it provocative.

One of the features that makes this book unique is right here in the introduction. We have included a short quiz for you to take. The quiz is designed to serve two basic purposes. First, the quiz is designed to test your "value quotient." How aware are you of important value concepts? How receptive and adaptive is your institution to change in the direction of a value orientation? By buying this book you have already indicated an openness and a willingness to learn more about the importance of identifying opportunities to create value for your customers. The quiz will raise some critical questions about how you see the current and future health of your institution and will help to identify factors to be addressed in order to maintain your bank's strategic health. You will notice that we have not provided the "correct answers." These are in the book. After reading the book you can score your own quiz.

Second, we have designed the quiz to be used in your bank as a "value audit." Make copies of the quiz and circulate it to your employees. Their collective response will give you some idea of how aware, receptive, and yes, how fearful they are concerning the need to adapt to the rapidly changing realities of operating a financial institution in today's competitive cauldron. Examining this "value audit" after you have read the book will provide you and your executive team with some very interesting information. The audit will provide you with insight into how to formulate or reformulate a vision statement, your bank's mission statement, and above all, some extremely useful and valuable information concerning you bank's culture—all in terms of customer value. It will force you to question the efficacy of your current philosophy and strategic approach to the different product/markets that you currently serve. It will challenge a number of operating assumptions that creep into your everyday management philosophy that may be detrimental to your bank's well-being.

For all readers, we are offering a unique service, and one which again differentiates our book from others. If you collect the information on the value audit from your employees and send it to us, we will compile it for you and send it back to you with information on how other peer institutions scored on the quiz.[1] There is no charge for this "value added" service. You will find it particularly useful in answering a number of questions that will normally arise in any candid conversation and discussion about the future of your institution. We are happy to provide this service for you.

Are you ready to take the quiz?

---

1. You can mail your information to: Reg Goeke, 281 Homan Avenue, State College, Pennsylvania 16801 (814/234-2486).

1. Which of the following words best describes the general nature of your bank's corporate culture?
    A. Cost conscious
    B. Sales oriented
    C. Market driven
    D. Customer value driven
    E. Other

2. How do you define customer value?
    A. Customer satisfaction is synonymous with customer value.
    B. Value is the ratio of benefits received for the price paid.
    C. Value is the same thing as customer service.
    D. Value is the ratio of customer satisfaction to the level of customer service.

3. In your bank, information gleaned from the income statement is equally as important as information obtained from market surveys.
    A. True
    B. False
    C. Don't know

4. The culture in your bank readily embraces innovation and change.
    A. True
    B. False
    C. Don't know

5. Customers in your market can clearly point to your bank as the top value provider of financial services.
    A. True
    B. False
    C. Don't know

6. Your bank has a clearly articulated and shared vision statement.
    A. True
    B. False
    C. Don't know

7. Opportunities to create customer value are:
    A. Universal
    B. Product/market specific
    C. Generated by a product development team
    D. Taken from banking magazines

8. On average, we conduct market surveys of our customers opinions every:
    A. Year
    B. Quarter
    C. Two years
    D. Whenever we think we need one.

9. There is no way to measure the value we deliver to our customers relative to the value delivered by our competitors.
    A. True
    B. False
    C. Don't know

10. I would characterize our organization as a:
    A. Typical bank
    B. Traditional organization
    C. Learning organization
    D. Sales organization

11. People in my bank would define our business as:
    A. Banking
    B. A business that provides financial services
    C. Financial problem solvers
    D. A place where customers can get checking accounts, savings accounts, etc.

12. I am personally familiar with the concept of alignment as it pertains to organizational behavior.
    A. True
    B. False

13. The top management of our bank is best described as:
    A. Innovative, open to new ideas
    B. Traditional bankers
    C. Resistant to change
    D. Unsure of the future of the industry

14. In my bank, every employee can put a dollar figure on the value of a customer.
    A. True
    B. False

15. Nonmanagement personnel in my bank are involved in decisions about cost and service.
    A. True
    B. False

16. We periodically examine the various service processes in our bank for redundancies and opportunities for faster service.
    A. True
    B. False

17. Customer retention is a priority in our bank.
    A. True
    B. False

18. Customer loyalty is directly related to:
    A. The level of service they receive
    B. The level of value they perceive
    C. The level of customer satisfaction they experience
    D. The fees we charge for various services

19. In our market(s), our bank probably gives a level of service that is:
    A. About average
    B. A little below average
    C. A little above average
    D. Way above average

20. People in my bank do not have fun in their work.
    A. True
    B. False

21. How well would your fellow employees say you listen to them?
    A. Not very well
    B. Adequately
    C. Attentively

22. Is your bank run on the basis of stacks and stacks of procedure manuals?
    A. Yes
    B. No

23. Is risk an accepted part of decision making?
    A. Yes
    B. No

24. Is intelligent failure accepted in your bank or is it treated as a mistake and the individual who failed is blamed?

     A. Yes

     B. No

25. Are the costs of nonchange clearly understood by your management team?

     A. Yes

     B. No

26. My bank considers employee training as:

     A. An investment

     B. An expense

27. We have a number of cross-functional teams in place to examine specific customer problems.

     A. True

     B. False

28. Tools such as value mapping, benchmarking, and half-life curves are frequently used in our bank to improve the value of our product/service offering.

     A. True

     B. False

1. TOWARD A NEW PHILOSOPHY OF BUSINESS

> "Put another way, reality has changed but the theory of business has not changed with it."
> -Peter Drucker

T hroughout the economic history of the United States we have witnessed the demise of once great industries and institutions. The railroads, once thought to be limitless in their future and their growth potential, succumbed to a series of events from which they have not been able to recover. The United States commercial shipping industry, once vibrant and powerful, is on the brink of slipping into nonexistence. More recently we have seen dramatic convulsions in such industry giants as Sears, IBM, Kmart, and other corporate stalwarts, which, only a few years ago seemed invincible. Are these changes inexorable and inevitable? Are these destructive perturbations built into the dynamics of organizational structure and industrial evolution? What causes these organizations and industries to stumble and lose the all important momentum that impels them to greatness? More to the point of this book, are we witnessing the same forces at work within the commercial banking industry?

Consider some of the symptoms of industrial malaise manifesting themselves in commercial banking. In a relatively short period of time we have seen the commercial banking industry evolve at warp speed from its position as a foundation of our free enterprise system to an industry that is in turmoil. It has gone from an industry with a clear and strong identity to a clearly schizoid industry searching for an identity amid a vast array of choices. Indeed, much of the argument concerning the industry focuses on whether it is a mature industry or an industry in decline. Symptomatic of this condition is intense competition with a heavy emphasis on price competition, typical of those industries suffering from overcapacity. A strong argument can be made that there are *too many banks* in this country. It is an industry in which product life cycles are greatly accelerated with less opened windows of profitability. Innovative product/service offerings are rapidly reduced to a commodity-like status where little, if any, differentiation exists. This lack of product differentiation is economically inhibiting in an industry attempting to move from an income source, driven principally by interest rates, to income generated from customers willing to pay fees for products and services that not long ago they received for free. Catalyzing this decline is a convenience of entry into selected profitable areas of the industry, some would argue, aided and abetted by a one-sided regulatory system which gives preference to credit unions, brokerage firms, and other extra-industrial competitors.

The effect of these conditions on the commercial banking industry was predictable. From 1986 to 1992, the industry has lost 80,000 jobs. There has been a 12-point drop in financial asset share held by the commercial banking industry in the 23-year period between 1970 and 1993.[1] During roughly this same period, the industry has lost nearly 3,500 banks to either merger or failure.[2]

These symptoms and results attest to a *failure of the current business philosophy* embraced by many commercial bank managements within the industry. In all fairness to these managements, the philosophy that has helped create the industry conditions of today is really an amalgam of a number of residual philosophies that have blown through the industry when the regulatory window was opened in the early 1980s.

It is not our contention that these philosophies have been misapplied or that bank managements are incompetent. In many instances, based on our own extensive consulting experience not only with commercial banks but other service and manufacturing firms as well, we have witnessed managements that have expertly and adroitly wielded the tools of these philosophies. It is our contention, however, that the current philosophy or confluence of philosophies is not appropriate for the nature of the commercial banking industry and is indeed potentially destructive. The current business philosophy of commercial banking no longer fits its operating reality.

IN SEARCH OF A PHILOSOPHY OF BUSINESS

Every organization, either implicitly or explicitly, embraces a philosophy of business. This philosophy is comprised of a set of beliefs and assumptions about how an organization interacts with its customers. An organization's philosophy of business dictates the way it does business.

Within a relatively short period of time, the commercial banking industry has been introduced to a number of different philosophies of business. The number and the rapidity with which these philosophies have been sold to the industry and diffused throughout it have occasioned more than one banker to express concern over the "flavor of the month" when it comes to a serious discussion of these philosophies. In their order of popularity or application, they would include a *production philosophy, sales philosophy, and market philosophy (with several different orientations, the first being a focus on customer service followed by a focus on customer satisfaction)*. Interacting with these various philosophies is a heavy regulatory mantle, weighing down upon bank managements, relegating strategic concerns to more tactical issues such as fair lending and community reinvestment. The effect of this regulation on strategic planning and strategic thinking is similar to driving a car by looking ahead only a few feet at a time instead of a mile down the road.

These philosophies, or philosophical hybrids, have certain assumptions embedded within which, when properly applied, have created and will continue to create the very symptoms we described earlier. It may prove useful to examine in brief the nature of these various philosophies and the limiting assumptions that drive them.

A Production Philosophy

This philosophy of business is a holdover from the pre-deregulation period of banking in which the demand for banking services and products was greater than the supply of them. It is a philosophy particularly suited for a seller's market.

With the huge expansion of the domestic economy in the aftermath of World War II, the commercial banking industry found itself in the highly enviable position of being the country's principal source of loans and capital. The pent-up demand for consumer goods, automobiles, and homes unleashed by returning GIs made selling of banking services unnecessary. Bankers were inside order takers with the attitude, "If you want money come see me." This is the fundamental operating assumption of a production philosophy. It emphasizes efficiency with its attendant concerns for standardization and uniformity while deemphasizing the idea that products or services have to match customer needs. A production philosophy directs management to offer as few types of products or services as possible, and to pound the round customers into the square holes.

Emphasis was on making money as readily available as possible. This was made easier by a regulatory environment which guaranteed profits through established interest spreads. Fee income was inconsequential. There were no concerns about the marketing of products or services. There were no concerns about pricing because bundling of costs and cross-subsidization of product/service offerings were the rules. There were few concerns about the customer. Bankers knew well what they were willing to offer the customer and were able to supply it with relative ease. The banking system was truly the wallet of the free enterprise system, fueling its expansion throughout the 1950s and into the 1960s.

Figure 1-1
FINANCIAL SHARE OF COMMERCIAL BANKS

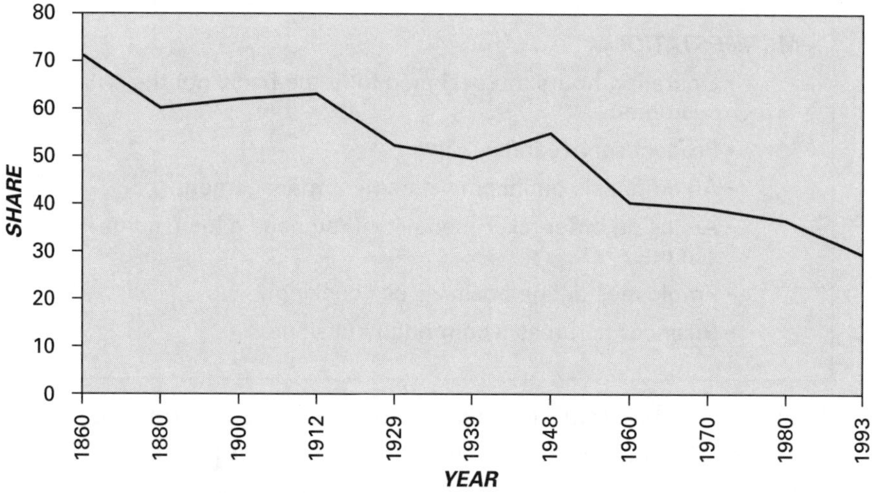

At about this same time (1948), the commercial banking industry controlled about 55.9 percent of all assets held by the various financial institutions in the United States (Figure 1-1). Its closest competitor was the insurance industry which held about 24.3 percent of the financial assets in this country. Thrift institutions collectively held about 12.3 percent of the assets; of these, 4.7 percent were held by savings and loans, 7.2 percent by savings banks, and only .2 percent by credit unions. Moreover, at this time the commercial banking industry was employing about 20 percent of all financial, insurance, and real estate workers.[3] These numbers truly reflect commercial banking's relative dominance within the financial services industry, driven by a reality which made the assumptions of a production philosophy appropriate.

5

Figure 1-2
KEY ASSUMPTIONS AND MANIFESTATIONS
OF A PRODUCTION PHILOSOPHY

ASSUMPTIONS:

- Mass production of product/service offerings. (Give them any color of check as long as they are green.)
- Standardization—one checking account fits all.
- Cost-minimization.

MANIFESTATIONS:

- Operating hours are designed to fit the bank, not the customer.
- Product/service inflexibility.
- An emphasis on income statement management.
- An inside order-taker mentality. (You need a loan, come see me.)
- Employees define business as "banking."
- Business is run as a commodity business.

It is remarkable that, because of the protected nature of the commercial banking industry with its guaranteed profit margins, this philosophy of business was the model that drove many commercial banks up to and into the 1980s, long after other firms in other business sectors had abandoned it for its inappropriateness (Figure 1-2). A production philosophy endured until a 1980s change in the regulatory environment made its governing assumptions obsolete and demanded a new business philosophy with new assumptions.

The Sales Philosophy

A sales philosophy attempts to respond to market realities that reverse the relationship between buyer and seller found in a production environment. That is, market conditions here are characterized by supply exceeding demand. The growth of the industry and the growth of competition, in part, spurred by deregulation, produced a market where many more competitors were operating.

Consumers had significantly greater choice and exercised that choice with a resulting partitioning of market share and profitability among many more diverse and capable competitors. Commercial banking found itself in this situation in the early days of the 1980s.

Indeed, it is this very loss of market share and profitability that dramatically signaled the need for a new business philosophy—an increased emphasis on sales. A fundamental assumption of the sales philosophy is that increased market share and profitability can be achieved through a greater selling and promotional effort (Figure 1-3). Banking schools and seminars sustained, reacted to, and reinforced this philosophy of business by offering programs to sharpen bankers' selling skills. Motivation of employees became a hot topic as bank managements sought ways to stimulate selling efforts. Short-term fixes were sought as the assumptions of a sales philosophy dictated greater individual selling effort on the part of bank officers and front-line workers who found their job descriptions rewritten, almost overnight.

Figure 1-3
KEY ASSUMPTIONS AND MANIFESTATIONS
OF A SALES PHILOSOPHY

ASSUMPTIONS:
- Loss of financial share is a result of a lack of selling effort.
- Increases in profitability come from increases in promotional effort (selling).
- Employees must be motivated and given incentive to sell.

MANIFESTATIONS:
- Hastily rewritten job descriptions.
- Increase in the number of motivational speeches and speakers in the bank.
- Commissions and incentives (the chance to eat dinner with the president of the bank).
- Increased emphasis on cross-selling.
- Increased emphasis on selling at banking schools.
- Business is defined as "we sell banking products."

The fallacy of this underlying assumption of the sales philosophy is that it ignores a fundamental marketplace reality—changing consumer needs. Instead, the assumption falsely directs management to redouble its selling efforts based on the premise that falling market share and profitability are neither the result of changing consumer needs nor poor product/service/customer matches resulting in value loss, but rather a lack of promotional effort.

It derives from a management that fails to understand the difference between the strategic health of the organization and its financial health. The former is a focus on the question "What kind of financial service institution do we need to be in two years or five years?" The latter poses the question "What kind of year did this bank have last year?" The dichotomy of financial health versus strategic health can easily be explained by looking at the responses to this changing reality made by a number of our banking clients.

Increasing competition provides greater customer choice. This was readily seen in the early days of deregulation when the DIDMCA took effect. Many of our bank clients saw S&Ls gaining significant amounts of market share based on a price competition. Bank managements responded to this competitive threat by reducing their fees and rates in an effort to neutralize what they perceived to be the S&L differential advantage. This competitive response proved costly for many banks resulting in a decline in profitability. How to increase profitability or at least stem the loss of profits became of paramount importance. The answer was readily apparent from an examination of the income statement. A significant cost component of commercial banks (indeed any service organization) is labor costs. Many bank managements fixed on this short-term response and began laying off employees. Downsizing and outsourcing became the trend. Between 1986 and 1992, 80,000 jobs were eliminated in the commercial banking industry.[4] Unfortunately, this focus on *financial health* ignored the more important and fundamental questions regarding the bank's *strategic health*.

As layoffs took place, customers began to experience lower and lower levels of customer service. A commodity industry where little, if any, product differentiation exists, where there are a myriad of choices for the customer, amplified by a demonstrable lack of concern for customer service or, at best, a concern relegated in importance to cost considerations, are three compelling reasons why customers should take their business elsewhere. And that is just what they did. Many value-creating activities were cut or eliminated resulting in a lack of competitiveness. The long-term strategic health of the business was sacrificed for the short-term financial health. A symptom was treated, but the illness was not cured.

If we examine the commercial banking industry's share of financial assets in the early 1980s, we see the effects of an emphasis on financial health. Share of industry financial assets dropped to 34.8 percent (down from 55.9 percent in 1948). Thrift institutions supplanted insurance companies as the most significant competitor. Their share of the industry's assets rose from 12.3 percent in 1948 to 21.4 percent in 1980. S&Ls accounted for 15.5 percent of the share. Looming on the horizon as a fierce competitor were investment companies which held a negligible share of assets in 1948. By 1980, they would control 3.6 percent of all financial assets, about one-tenth of the share of commercial banks.[5]

Rather than focusing solely on the financial health of the bank, managements should have been asking some crucial and critically important strategic health questions. "What kind of organization do we need to be one year, three years, or five years from now to be successful?" "What kind of business philosophy do we need to embrace to be successful?" "What is it that customers want and need from a financial institution that they are not getting now?" These are the types of questions that force an organization to focus on strategic health. They are the types of questions that underlie a different philosophy of business, a market philosophy .

9

Consider, for a moment, how Taco Bell CEO, John E. Martin dealt with a similar situation in the fast-food industry. In 1983, Mr. Martin was faced with a changing reality that was impelling Taco Bell into becoming a declining regional restaurant. How he reversed this situation by concentrating on strategic health clearly shows the difference and the importance of that focus relative to a sole concentration on financial health. His first step, and perhaps his most important step, was not to follow competition by attempting to bring down the cost of goods sold. Rather, he decided to maintain the quality of his food but to reduce the costs of everything else, including his marketing costs. What were the effects of this focus on strategic health? In 10 years he has taken Taco Bell from a $500 million, 1,800 site chain to an enterprise consisting of over 4,500 locations earning more than $3.9 billion with an eye to increasing sales to $20 billion by the year 2000.[6]

The Market Philosophy

While commercial banking was attempting to extricate itself from an outdated business philosophy, many other firms were coming to grips with the fundamental success proposition that is embedded within the market philosophy. A market philosophy presupposes that a firm pays attention to and gets its signals from the marketplace. Customers know what they want and will reward those firms that provide it. No longer can product decisions, distribution decisions, pricing decisions, and promotional decisions be made in the boardroom, in an absence of customer input. The strategic, and ultimately, the financial health of the organization depend directly on the organization's ability to understand what customers want and to provide it better than their competitors.

There have been two major evolving orientations within this market philosophy of business. The first is the emphasis on customer service. In a commodity industry with many competitors and undifferentiated products, customer service becomes the *sine qua non* of competition. By failing to differentiate product offerings, bank managements rightly turned their attention to ways in which they could provide superior service to their customers.

Figure 1-4
KEY ASSUMPTIONS AND MANIFESTATIONS
OF A MARKET PHILOSOPHY

ASSUMPTIONS:

- The customer knows what they want and will reward the bank that can provide it the best.
- Product/service decisions can no longer be made in the absence of customer input.
- There are many alternatives for banking product/service offerings.
- The supply of product/service offerings exceeds the demand for them.

MANIFESTATIONS:

- Increased emphasis on marketing research.
- Increased training on skills such as customer service.
- Increased emphasis on fee income.
- Lots of talk about customers, but not enough action.

This service philosophy was forced on the commercial banking industry by outside competitive forces. During the late 1980s and early 1990s, many firms were realizing the importance of providing outstanding customer service to their customers. Customers increasingly were able to get faster, more attentive and more convenient service from restaurants, airlines, grocery stores, and retailers. Why couldn't they get it from banks? In fact, outside industry competitors such as Southwest Airlines, Taco Bell, Xerox, and Federal Express set the standards for service that banks were forced to adopt. Again, commercial banking found itself in a reactive mode.

A few banks were quick to see the advantage that outstanding customer service could provide them. Northern Trust in Chicago leveraged their legacy of a strong customer service orientation so successfully that they were able to make the claim that 55 percent of their operating profits were generated from fees. This was an unheard of result testifying to the ability of service to impact profits. Seafirst in Seattle, Washington used a focus on customer service to become the dominant retail institution in the Northwest. Concord Commercial Bank in Concord, California drives its commercial business on its ability to provide outstanding customer service to its clients.

While there have been some notable successes, there have been many bankers who have been less than satisfied by the customer service orientation. They are not seeing the promised gains in profitability made by customer service gurus. Why?

The answer, we believe, is that customer service is a *process*, not an *outcome*. Many banks have become slaves to their focus on the process rather than on the outcome, which is the creation of customer satisfaction. Quality became a buzzword, but as every bank claimed that it was providing quality service, customer ratings of their banks fell. Deed did not match claim. In fact, in a 1992 study conducted by the *American Banker*, 36 percent of credit union members surveyed said that service had improved over the last year as opposed to only 19 percent of their bank counterparts.[7]

The outcome that is desired is satisfaction. Increased customer service is the process by which customers are to be satisfied. However, even this refinement in thinking begs a fundamental question. Satisfied with what? The current thinking suggests that customers want to be satisfied with faster, friendlier and more responsive service. Based on our work with different companies and banks, we have come to another conclusion. Customers want to be satisfied with the value delivered by their bank. A brief example will make this point clearer.

Assume that a customer applies for a mortgage at the Friendliest Bank in Town. The bank offers a mortgage at a reasonable interest rate with one point and a half point origination fee. The customer feels that this is good value and completes the paperwork. One day later the same customer learns about a mortgage package from a competitive bank at the same interest rate, no points and no origination fee. Our customer is no longer satisfied with the value proposition offered by The Friendliest Bank in Town. The competitor has created a greater value proposition.

Satisfaction is an emotional response to a value comparison. To create satisfied customers a bank has to offer outstanding value. Focusing on satisfaction by trying to be more responsive or friendlier misplaces strategic focus. Focus must be on the ability of the bank to offer greater customer value than any other financial service provider.

Many bank managements do not understand this relationship between value and satisfaction and have spent much time and effort trying to get employees to be friendlier, more courteous, faster, and more responsive without any significant impact on the bottomline. It is value that leads to satisfaction, in turn producing the customer retention capabilities that lead to greater profitability.

Service quality, in addition, fails to acknowledge an extremely important fact in a commodity business, price. This is the cost customers pay for their service quality and/or other benefits that lead to satisfaction. Customer service at a high customer cost is not satisfying for most customers. Customer satisfaction is dependent upon value, where value is viewed as the perceived quality relative to price, or benefits received relative to costs incurred. Customer satisfaction cannot be divorced from the price customers pay for it. Quality, however, is not dependent upon price. The mistake that bank managements made was to erroneously construe quality to mean customer satisfaction.

In addition, most banks were managed from their financial statements and were not really dedicated to the delivery of outstanding customer satisfaction in the first place. While many bankers will deny the superficiality of customer satisfaction efforts, customers will readily attest to it. These two weaknesses of the customer satisfaction philosophy, lack of commitment on the part of bank managements to implement and manage customer satisfaction and failure to incorporate price into the delivery of satisfaction neutered it as a competitive weapon. The efficacy of this poorly implemented philosophy was ultimately born out by a continual decline in financial assets.

Between 1980 and 1993, the industry experienced close to a 10 percent decline in its share of financial assets. As of 1993 the commercial banking industry controlled about 25.4 percent of the financial assets, down from 55.9 percent in 1948, 38.2 percent in 1960, 37.9 percent in 1970. The apparent beneficiary of this declining share position is investment companies who over the same time period (1980–1993) increased their share from 3.6 percent (1980) to 14.9 percent (1993). Pension funds also enjoyed a significant amount of growth during this same period. Their share of the market increased from 17.4 percent in 1980 to 24.4 percent in 1993. Commercial bankings' old nemesis, thrifts, lost share from 21.4 percent in 1980 to 7.4 percent in 1993.[8]

What accounted for this shift in relative and absolute positions? When commercial banking was attempting to provide faster, friendlier, and more responsive service to its customers, why was it continually hemorrhaging market share to such likely competitors as investment companies, insurance companies and credit unions, and such unlikely competitors as phone companies and automobile companies?

What we have learned from our work with various banks and other service industries is that *customer value* is the critical customer benefit and hence the driver of such crucial performance measures as customer retention and profitability. *Understanding the importance of customer value means also understanding that creating customer value is the objective of the bank, profitability or performance then becomes an outcome of achieving this objective.* This is the essence of the difference between the strategic health of the bank and its financial health.

Banks have been slow to respond to the increasing demand for customer value. They have been overtrumped by AT&T, Merrill

Lynch, GM, and credit unions, to name but a few. While offering the same customer value, or at least making the claim, other competitors have raised the stakes. It remains to be seen whether commercial banking can respond to this new and changing reality.

CUSTOMER VALUE—THE NEW PHILOSOPHY

What customers want to be satisfied with is value. Value is driving their decisions about where to shop, where to eat, what to wear, where to vacation, and who is going to provide their financial service needs. The prophetic importance of customer value and its impact on performance is extremely well articulated in the following statement about competition in the 1990s:

> Those firms that do not provide value, by inability, inattention, or choice, will be selectively eliminated by the customer at the point of purchase. The implications are clear: The organization's objectives in the twenty-first century will be to become increasingly valued by the users of their products or services, and this principle holds for both industrial and consumer goods.[9]

As a benchmark, how are different firms beginning to respond to this new value directive? One example from an industry that is not dissimilar to commercial banking is the grocery business. In the past five years, consumers have increasingly forsaken the glitz of nationally advertised grocery products for the more value-laden store brands. A report issued by the Private Label Manufacturer Association in March of 1994 clearly attests to the power of providing customers with value. Market share of store brands climbed to a record high of 19.7 percent compared with a share of 16.4 percent in 1989. Dollar share climbed to 14.9 percent, up from 11.6 percent in 1989. Grocers are responding to this increased need for value by improving their private label programs in an attempt to extend their value, according to Brian Sharnoff, president of the Private Label Association in New York.[10]

Recall, if you will, John Martin's approach to revitalizing Taco Bell. His emphasis was on providing greater quality at lower customer

15

cost. Mr. Martin was clearly focusing on delivering superior value to his customers. Not to be outdone, McDonalds responded to Taco Bell's success with superior value by launching its own "extra-value meals" by increasing the size of the meals and offering them at lower prices. According to fast-food experts this move "will put more pressure on McDonald's fast-food competitors in an environment that's become quite price-sensitive and value oriented."[11]

How is Taco Bell handling the "pressure"? Mr. Martin's response is to reinvent Taco Bell with the express purpose of delivering greater value to its customers. Out of every dollar spent by a customer at Taco Bell, Mr. Martin wants that customer to receive 40 cents worth of food. This is remarkable in an industry where the current average is 27 cents.[12] It attests to the importance of value as a strategic weapon.

The pizza business is feeling the effects of the "value war" that is breaking out in the fast-food business. According to one industry consultant, Ronald Paul, consumers are now perceiving greater value in burger meals resulting in a slowing down in sales for the once fast growing pizza segment.[13]

Not to be outdone, "casual dining" restaurants are understanding the importance of customer value. These are niche type restaurants, positioned between fast-food operations and expensive upscale restaurants. Derek Jones, Director of Prudential Equity Investors, New York notes, "Consumers are looking for high-quality restaurant products that are also great value. Casual-dining operators have been aggressive in addressing this need."[14]

A former client of ours is yet another example of the power of customer value. Kmart conducted a leadership conference in which we participated over the past several years. One of the authors developed an exceptional module focusing on the opportunities and challenges that a constantly changing retail environment provides. In this module, he engages Kmart managers to examine what has happened to Kmart and Wal-mart since their inceptions in 1962. After reaching a conclusion about the basic performance drivers in the discount retail business, quality and price, the managers set about examining how customers have perceived the two giant competitors during the past decade relative to these two attributes. Every class reaches the same conclusion. Kmart has not been able to deliver the same customer value that Wal-mart has. The increasing distance between the two retailers on the position maps that the Kmart managers develop shows a significant perceived diminution in the relative quality of the offering of Kmart with respect to that of Wal-mart. In addition, the effect of Wal-mart's EDLP (every day low prices) policy makes the value proposition at Wal-mart even that much more salient than that of Kmart's. The conclusion of Kmart managers: Wal-mart provides a more value-laden shopping experience than does Kmart! What would happen if you conducted a similar exercise at your bank?

Even in an industry driven by glitz, emotion, and high prices, customer value is finding a welcome audience. The cosmetics industry is redirecting its appeals to women, changing from its business as usual to a more value-driven approach ushered in by the changing reality. Industry leaders are seeing a consumer who is more intelligent than in the past. Rosie Albright, vice-president of marketing for Clinique's new Almay product states, "She's reading labels, she understands how ingredients work, she wants products that truly perform." This change to a more value-laden product is driven by a fundamental change in the reality of the business. Ms. Albright notes, "In the 1990s, even people with very high incomes are very price conscious.[15]"

Not even venerable old Rolls Royce has been immune from the increasing emphasis on value. Rolls has been hit hard by customers demanding increased value during the 1990s. Sales of Rolls in the United States fell from 1,200 cars in 1990 to only 341 in 1993.[16]

In a commodity industry like forest products, customer value has become a strong competitive weapon. Traditionally, the chief competitive weapon in the forest products industry has been price. Customer value had been created by offering the same quality of

17

product, but at lower prices. Price competition ruled. "Today, to some degree, virtually all forest products companies understand that they can create superior value for buyers of commodities on a basis other than price."[17]

The emerging importance of value was communicated to one of the authors by Mrs. Lefkowitz, an elderly woman, and, as it turned out extremely sagacious participant in a focus group concerning the viability of a new banking product. Mrs. Lefkowitz gave meaning to the George Bernard Shaw quote, "Common sense is instinct. Enough of it is genius."

In an attempt to understand the price sensitivity of customers to a new banking product, the focus group was asked to react to a set of price alternatives. Mrs. Lefkowitz had remained silent throughout most of the discussion. At one point she was asked point blank, "Mrs. Lefkowitz, would you pay $6.00 per month for this product at your bank?" She responded, "Why should I pay $6.00 for crappy service when I can already get it for $2.00?" Common sense blossomed into genius, and it put into perspective what value was all about.

Commercial banking must learn to respond to this new reality of business. They must take to heart the admonishment of Mrs. Lefkowitz. Individual banks must adopt a philosophy of business with its attendant assumptions that recognizes and is driven by customer value. To ignore this changing reality and continue with an outdated philosophy will surely hasten its march to irrelevance and insignificance.

Every bank must redefine its philosophy of business around three guiding tasks. Commercial banks must learn to:

1. *identify value opportunities* in specific product/markets;

2. *create value* for specific product/markets; and

3. *maintain or sustain value relationships* within those specific product/markets.

Reality is clearly focused on *the competition for sustainable value differentiation*. This is the core of the new value philosophy of commercial banking. Those banks that master the tools and techniques of this value philosophy will be in a position to leverage their differential value advantage into superior performance and long-term survivability.

The remainder of this book focuses on the design and implementation of a value philosophy. We will show how to use the tools of customer value analysis, how to implement a philosophy of business driven by the creation of customer value and ultimately, how to sustain differential value advantages for your bank.

Endnotes

1. Kaufman, George G. and Larry R. Mote (1994) "Is Banking a Declining Industry? A Historical Perspective." *Economic Perspectives* (May/June). Federal Reserve Bank of Chicago, p. 7.

2. Federal Deposit Insurance Corporation.

3. Kaufman and Mote, p. 7.

4. Kaufman and Mote, p. 7.

5. Kaufman and Mote, p. 7.

6. ———. (1994) "Ringing Up Sales at Taco Bell" *Personal Selling Power*, Vol. 14, No. 6, Fredricksburg, VA, p. 51.

7. Caruthers, Chrystal (1994) "Credit Unions Step It Up", *The Sun Herald* (September 25), p. E1.

8. Kaufman and Mote, p. 7.

9. Elliot, Stuart (1994) "Advertising" the *New York Times*, (March 22).

10. *Ibid.*

11. ———. (1994) "Big Mac Taking Bite Out of Meal Prices", *The Clarion Ledger* (July 2), p. 6B.

12. Crain, Rance (1994) "Taco Bell Again Poised to Chisel Away Costs" *Advertising Age* (September 12).

13. Goldman, Kevin (1994) "Pizza Chains Want a Bigger Piece of Pie" *The Wall Street Journal* (June 6), p. B4.

14. Gupta, Udayan (1994) "Classier 'Casual Dining' Restaurants are Expanding" *The Wall Street Journal* (July 6), p. B2.

15. Hwang, Suein L. (1994) "Make Up Ads Downplay Glamour for Value" *The Wall Street Journal* (June 20), p. B6.

16. ———. (1994) "A Racy Rolls" *Fortune* (July 25), p. 17.

17. Narver, John C. and Stanley Slater (1990) "The Effect of a Market Orientation on Business Profitability" *Journal of Marketing* (October), p. 27.

2. The Value Equation

> "Every generation needs a revolution."
> -*Thomas Jefferson*

I n Chapter 1 we pointed out and demonstrated how the fundamental reality of commercial banking has changed. We argued that what is needed is a new business philosophy —a philosophy based on the concept of customer value. In this chapter we will examine the value equation, several value properties, and look, in some detail, at what we call value propositions. These are the fundamental underpinnings of value that make it such a potent competitive weapon.

A number of environmental factors are impelling commercial banks to embrace a value orientation. Perhaps the most compelling factor is the significant change in consumer behavior that is shaping corporate responses. This value orientation is further catalyzed by a relentlessly changing technological environment offering lower cost options that can be translated into lower customer prices. But perhaps the most formidable force shaping commercial banking strategic alternatives is a hyper competitive environment, laden with new and powerful competitors. These competitors have honed their skills in the competitive crucibles of consumer markets where customers are not just kings, they are dictators. By bringing these skills to bear on the financial services industry, they are enjoying a considerable learning advantage over their more traditional counterparts. This is an advantage that can only be neutralized with a new approach to the market, one driven by a focus on customer value.

THE VALUE EQUATION

There are a number of different meanings for the word value. There is the value that is used to describe a set of standards that are held by a certain group or class of people. Value is also used in the sense of "value added," referring to the incremental utility that is added at various stages of the production or distribution process. When we speak of value we are referring to a specific type of value, a value-in-exchange.

Value-in-exchange is a very powerful concept. Value has the capacity to explain why entire industries decline and fail. It has the ability to explain why corporate giants stumble and fall. Value can explain decisions to move production facilities offshore and it can explain the rise in the relatively recent phenomenon of outsourcing. In all cases, customers are constantly seeking better value—be it from other industries, other companies, other countries, other suppliers, or other organizations than their own.

Most people have an intuitive understanding of the concept of value in exchange. We hear expressions such as "more bang for our buck," "it's a real bargain," or "it's really worth it." In south Louisiana there is a Cajun word called "lagniappe" (lanyap) which means a little bit extra for the same price, a similar concept to "a baker's dozen." All of these expressions connote the central idea of value.

The concept of value has been formally represented by the following expression:

$$VALUE = \frac{UTILITY}{PRICE}$$

Utility is that elusive measure of benefit invented by economists that confounds most beginning business students. The denominator of the expression is the cost of obtaining that utility. We can express the notion of value in somewhat more user-friendly terms such as:

$$VALUE = \frac{BENEFITS\ SOUGHT\ BY\ THE\ CUSTOMER}{PRICE\ CUSTOMER\ PAYS\ TO\ ACQUIRE\ BENEFITS}$$

This definition brings us closer to a more meaningful expression of value. In many cases benefits can be overt, clearly measurable, or observable factors such as weight or quantity. A pound of raw chocolate that costs $1.00 is a better value than a half-pound of raw chocolate at the same price. A bushel of peaches costing $5.00 is better than a peck of peaches costing $5.00. If we wanted a strong wire and, if the cost of wire were held constant, the wire with the greater tensile strength would be the better value.

In the marketing of services it is common to find benefits expressed in terms such as accessibility, responsiveness, satisfaction, and quality. These benefits are not easily measurable. Moreover, in many cases they are perceptual in nature.

If we view value as the relationship between the relative perceived quality of a bank's services and the relative prices that it charges customers for those services, we can identify a number of value trade-off options that have important significance for better understanding the dynamics of value creation. Value trade-off options are shown in Table 2-1.

The implications of the various trade-offs shown in the table are very important. For example, if we are currently offering a service that is perceived as being low in quality, or if our bank is presently known for its low quality of services, the most we can leverage from a manipulation of the price component of value is an average value position. Clearly, an average value position does not have the differentiating capabilities to catapult the bank into a position to enjoy the superior performance that a superior differential value advantage offers.

Table 2-1
RELATIVE QUALITY/RELATIVE PRICE TRADEOFFS
For Value Options

RELATIVE QUALITY/ RELATIVE PRICE	LOW	AVERAGE	HIGH
High	Inferior Value	Poor Average	Average Better
Average	Poor Value	Average Value	Better Value
Low	Average Value	Better Value	Superior Value

More typical of many banks is a second scenario where they are known for average quality of services. In this case the bank can manipulate the price component of the value equation and, at best, move to a better value situation.

The quality/price trade-off table makes salient the importance of providing high quality services and products. It is only those institutions that can provide this kind of quality for which a superior value option is available. And, it is only those institutions that can achieve this differential value advantage that will be able to enjoy the rewards of superior performance. The trade-off table makes it abundantly clear that in order to achieve a differential value advantage, the bank must do two things: Increase customer perceptions of its quality and drive out all costs not associated with the delivery of quality products and services. Lower costs must then be translated into a price advantage perceived by the customer.

VALUE PROPERTIES

The previously described definition of value has several important implications for commercial bankers. First, and most importantly, value is customer defined. Put another way, value, like beauty, is in the eyes of the customer. Value is not a term that is defined in the bank's boardroom or in the president's office. It originates and exists in the mind of the customer. It is incumbent upon all the bank's employees to understand, as clearly as possible, what customers consider important in their banking relationship. The strength of value as a competitive weapon is directly related to the clarity of understanding that the bank has of what benefits the customers think are important.

Second, value is perceptual in nature. This confounds many bankers who live in what they consider to be a very realistic number-dominated world. With respect to customer value, however, it is not too strong a statement to say that perception is more important than reality. If you find this hard to believe consider the following.

In the battle for competitive dominance between Kmart and Wal-mart, perception has played an important role. Both retail giants continually monitor the pricing of the other to guarantee that prices are not only in line with the competitor, but are nearly identical. Individuals from each store can be seen roaming the aisles of their competitors gathering information on prices. However, Wal-mart has made such a strong case for its EDLP (every day low prices) that most customers believe Wal-mart has significantly lower prices.

Similarly, if you ask customers of the two retailers who has the better exchange policy, typically you will hear that Wal-mart has the best, in spite of the reality that Kmart will actually refund money on purchases bought at Wal-mart but returned to Kmart! Kmart is clearly losing the battle of perceptions.

Where do customers learn about value? There are two main sources that are manageable by the bank: each customer's experience with the bank and the experiences of other customers with the bank. First, many customers learn about the value you deliver first hand. Every transaction completed or attempted in your bank carries a value message with it. Value is learned over time, and that is why it is so difficult to change or unlearn. This is particularly true for product/service categories that have important experience attributes. Experience attributes are those attributes that must be experienced by the customer in order for a value-in-use expectation to be formed. There are a number of banking product/services that fall into this category, especially those that have a financial return associated with them, and those that rely upon a service commitment from the bank. It is not entirely possible to judge the value of an investment in a certain product or service without actually experiencing the effects of that investment. Partial value judgments can be formed on the perception of the value. These partial judgments are augmented by judgments derived from experience. Nor is it possible to verify the value of a claim of superior service without actually experiencing that service.

For those product/services that have credence attributes (those attributes that may be more difficult to evaluate and that force the customer to rely on product/service or bank reputation for evaluation), customer perception of value may be directly formed or impacted by individuals outside the bank. Customers do not have to experience a situation to evaluate a bank or product/service on the basis of credence attributes. They can rely on information provided by other customers. For example, the TARP (Technical Assistance Research Project) studies conclude that, on average, a dissatisfied customer will tell a disparaging story about a negative incident to about nine other individuals:[1] Are your customers value apostles, spreading the word about the tremendous customer value delivered by your bank, or are they value terrorists, sabotaging your efforts to persuade customers about the value-laden relationship you are providing? Word-of-mouth advertising is an incredibly potent source of credence attributes. Your bank's reputation for delivering customer value is directly affected by these credence attributes, and if negative, can have a detrimental impact on customer retention and acquisition.

One final word about the source of value information. There is a process of value deterioration. We know that customers undergo an updating or learning process with respect to their evaluation of value. This process is much slower for the bank that is trying to improve its reputation for value. It takes much longer to improve on your value position than it does to lose it. By the same token the cumulative effect of this updating is more rapid for the bank that is losing its value position. This means that for the bank that is not paying attention to the value it is delivering to its customers, it will be significantly more difficult to teach customers that you do offer outstanding value after you have spent time teaching them that value was not important in the past. Playing catch up in the competition for value differentiation is both expensive and very time-consuming.

Finally, as the value equation points out, value can be increased by either increasing the perceived benefits that the customer receives or by reducing the costs the customer must pay to receive those benefits. In our experience as consultants to the industry, the emphasis on customer satisfaction has focused on increasing the benefits of the banking transaction, as perceived by the bank, but has ignored the costs the customer has paid to receive those benefits.

VALUE PROPOSITIONS

This brings us to a discussion of what we call value propositions, those fundamental propositions that make value the potent competitive weapon that it is. There are, we believe, six basic value propositions.

Value Proposition 1: The existence and perception of value are necessary conditions in any exchange situation.

It goes without saying, but we will say it anyway. Customers must perceive existing value in a situation in order for an exchange to take place. Currently, most commercial banks are giving their customers average value—or at least, this is the customer perception. Ask a group of bankers how they would honestly rate the level of service that they are giving their customers and the majority would respond "good," but not excellent. If everyone is providing their customers with good service then good is only average. Assuming nonsignificant differences in fee and rate schedules in any given market, commercial bank customers are probably getting average value.

This is survivable in the short run as long as no competitor, traditional or nontraditional, ups the value ante. But as we have shown in Chapter 1 that is exactly what is happening. Nontraditional competitors have upped the value ante, and many commercial banks have been the victims of this increased value competition. Average will no longer work. The reality of commercial banking has changed and a major component of this new reality is customer value. For those banks that choose not to compete on value, they will face increasing customer defections as their former customers perceive greater value in the competitive offerings of other financial service institutions. Relationships will hinge on the fragile and tenuous ability of your bank to deliver outstanding value to an increasingly spoiled, fickle, and sophisticated customer.

The harbinger of this type of competition may be seen in the battles of AT&T and MCI. Both communication companies are locked in an intensive competition over customer retention and acquisition. New programs and services are continually offered to not only maintain the value advantage that one company has achieved over the other, but also to increase the value advantage. It is a relentless battle for a differential value advantage.

Value Proposition 2: Some banks will be better able to identify, create, and maintain value opportunities than other banks.

Proposition 2 acknowledges the fact that some banks will have the management capability to achieve a competitive differential value advantage while others will not. Consider the two following cases.

Commercial bankers have been made acutely aware of the drain of dollars from CDs into mutual fund investments as customers discover greater value in these alternative investments. However, not all bankers have been willing to sit by and blame interest rate changes that are beyond their control. Bank Leumi Trust in New York has developed a value-added product called the Triple Choice Time Deposit (TCTD) that has many of the attractive attributes of a traditional CD—proximity, safety, and relative liquidity but have augmented the product with several value-added benefits. Typical

CDs require the customer to lock in a sum of money at a fixed rate for a specified period of time. The TCTD that has a two-year maturity and allows the customer to bump up the interest rate to a higher market rate one time during the investment period. Moreover, once during the two-year maturity period the customer can also withdraw up to 50 percent of the balance without penalty, and the customer can also add up to 100 percent of his or her initial deposit whenever he or she likes.

Other banks are providing their own version of this value added approach. For example, First Financial Bank in Milwaukee offers a 2-1/2 year CD with an initial annual interest payout of 5.35 percent that increases .75 percent every six months. Each increase permits the customer to withdraw or add to the account without penalty. First National Bank of Omaha has developed a two-tiered 20-month CD product that jumps from a 5.5 percent interest rate to 7 percent after 10 months.[2]

These products clearly demonstrate several bank's attempts at creating a differential value advantage. By increasing the benefits that the product offers (flexibility and increased payout), and decreasing the customer costs of obtaining those benefits (no penalty for withdrawal, for example), these banks have significantly enhanced the value of their CD product offerings.

Another example of a company that demonstrates the importance of Value Proposition 2 is in a related field. Progressive Corporation made money in the auto insurance business by charging risky drivers an above market priced premium. Both competition and regulation, however, conspired to force Peter Lewis, Progressive's chairman, CEO, and president to find a new way to make money. The thinking that gave rise to the new value-added approach went something like this. "People get screwed seven ways from Sunday in auto insurance," said Lewis. "They get dealt with adversarially, and they get dealt with slowly. Why don't we just stop that? Why don't we start dealing with them nicely? It would be a revolution in the business."[3]

The result of this thinking was the Immediate Response program, and the basis for a significant differential value advantage. Through a combination of technology and sheer hustle, Progressive provides an around-the-clock service to accident victims. This new program boasts of making contact with 80 percent of accident victims in less than nine hours of learning of the accident. Progressive's adjusters inspect 70 percent of the vehicles within one-day of the accident, and settle most collision damage within one week. Customers, who are typically dazed, anxious, scared, and traumatized, are met at the scene of the accident and ushered into an air-conditioned van equipped with comfortable chairs and cellular phones. Progressive's agent is on the spot offering advice on repair, medical care, police reports, and in many cases, is able to settle the claim before the accident site has been cleared.[4]

Progressive Corporation is an excellent example of a company that has eschewed the old philosophy of business and embraced the idea of creating customer value. They have established a differential value advantage. Customer benefits have been increased significantly, especially relative to those offered by other auto insurers who operate under the assumption that business as usual will work. This type of identification, creation, and maintenance of value opportunities eventually forces other competitors into a follow-the-leader position, and relegates them to a position of follower performance.

Value Proposition 3: Value opportunities are product/market specific.

Proposition 3 identifies the arena in which specific value opportunities are to be found. To better understand this proposition it is necessary to rethink the nature of competition in the financial services industry.

For many bankers, competition is thought to exist at the bank level. Many bankers conceptualize competition as taking place between their bank and another bank. In part this is true.

However, to think in these terms is too global and occludes the more exacting nature of competition.

Banks compete for a differential value advantage in the interaction of a product/market. The product (or service) is a revenue generating extension of the bank, and the market is the source of that revenue. Other banks, and other financial service competitors, with their own product/service mixes, are also competing for the same sources of revenue. That is, each product/market represents the competitive arena for a differential value advantage.

Each product/market will react differently to bank product/service offerings. Individual product/markets will have differing definitions, and resultant perceptions of value, of the various bank offerings. This means that your institution has to closely study and understand the benefits customers in a specific product/market consider to be the most important, and what costs they are willing to incur to acquire those benefits.

Returning to the premise of Value Proposition 2, some banks will be better able to do this than other banks. The ones that are the most capable will be the ones that are able to leverage this differential value advantage into superior performance. Value Proposition 3 is so important to our customer value philosophy that we are going to dedicate Chapter 5 to an in-depth discussion of how the product/market matrix will allow bankers to more clearly identify value opportunities, and how to exploit them.

Value Proposition 4: The bank that can identify, create, and maintain a differential value advantage will be in a stronger position to leverage that advantage into superior performance.

Throughout our discussion we have pointed to the relationship between a differential value advantage and superior performance. Our point has been that those banks that can achieve a differential value advantage in critical product/markets will be able to leverage this position into superior performance.

How does a differential value advantage affect an organization's performance? It does so in a number of ways. The organizations that provide superior value to their customers typically enjoy greater customer loyalty, experience reduced price elasticities for products and services, have lower costs of customer acquisition, and enjoy an enhanced reputation. Let's look at each of these factors.

Customer Retention

First, those firms enjoying a differential value advantage typically boast of greater customer loyalty. Customer loyalty translates into greater customer retention and increased product/service relationships, that, in turn, impacts bank profitability. Taco Bell cites the benefits of increased customer loyalty and retention by maintaining that a typical Taco Bell customer is worth $11,000 over the course of his or her life. Sewell Cadillac in Dallas points out that a satisfied customer is worth over $300,000.[5] Kmart makes the point that a satisfied Kmart customer is worth $75,000 over the course of his or her life. Finally, Frank Meeks, owner of 53 Domino's franchises in and around the Washington DC/Northern Virginia area claims a satisfied Domino's customer is worth about $21,000 over the customer's life.[6]

These are staggering numbers. They are made even more salient by understanding that in banking, customer acquisition costs are running about three to five times the costs of customer retention. Thus, not only are there revenue benefits from increased customer loyalty, but so too are there significant cost benefits. Together they provide superior profit potential for the bank that can achieve that all important differential value advantage.

For banking, customer relationships are of paramount importance. Banks spend significant amounts of time, money, and energy in attempting to increase the number of product/service purchases by each customer. Typically, the greater the relationship achieved, the greater the loyalty and the greater the customer retention rate.

The number one reason for customers switching banks is because they are not receiving the quality of service that they think they should. The typical defecting customer takes with him or her, on average, a three product relationship and a deposit balance of $23,000.[7] This represents a significant cost to the bank and one that is avoidable if the customer perceives value in his or her relationship with the bank.

Reduced Price Elasticities

Reduced price elasticities are a second benefit of a differential value advantage that has a positive impact on the bottom line of a bank. Reduced price elasticities were a major finding of the PIMS studies (Profit Impact of Marketing Studies). These studies found that the correlation between quality and selling price is indeed powerful. Firms that have achieved a superior quality position earned prices 8 percent higher than their counterparts that fell into the inferior quality category. In this same study it was found that increased quality was also directly responsible for reduced direct costs.[8] Reduced costs resulted from not having to do the same task over to correct it. Combining higher prices with lower direct costs yields greater profitability. This becomes attainable only for those firms providing sufficient value to enjoy a differential value advantage.

For many banks, increasing fee income is a strategic focus. As reported earlier, Northern Trust in Chicago is in the enviable position of earning about 55 percent of its operating income from noninterest sources. We estimate that for most banks noninterest income may account for no more than about 15 percent to 20 percent of it operating income. We are also seeing banks forced into the position of initiating charges for certain products that, only a few years ago, they gave away. Customer reaction to this change in pricing policy is predictable. They are highly resistant to it. However, for the bank that can establish a differential value advantage customers are less resistant to increases in fees, as long as there is a concomitant increase in the perceived benefits that they receive. To embark upon a policy of increasing prices without a perceived increase in benefits is to diminish the perceived value that customers receive.

Since most customers demonstrate some sensitivity to price and quality in their purchase decisions, a premium pricing strategy may have an adverse effect on such performance measures as increased product usage and market share. Furthermore, in many instances, performance measures such as ROI (return on investment) are actually higher for those firms that have kept their prices at a moderate level or below that of their competition while improving quality. This has been especially true in those industries characterized by uniform and undifferentiated product/service offerings, certainly characteristics of the commercial banking industry. The PIMS studies also reveal that firms in low growth industries, again like commercial banking, can benefit the most from enhancing product value.

Customer Acquisition

While customer retention is rightfully receiving quite a bit of attention these days, customer acquisition remains important. We reported earlier that customer acquisition costs are running about three to five times customer retention costs. A bank that can establish a clear differential value advantage has the ability to acquire customers at a lower cost than its competitors.

As we pointed out earlier, the major tactical weapon in customer acquisition is a satisfied current customer. These customers can act as apostles for your bank, telling other customers of their satisfaction. This can enhance the effectiveness of your advertising and increase its credibility, thereby accruing greater promotional returns.

The PIMS studies also revealed a strong relationship between quality changes and market share positions. This relationship may not be as pronounced in commercial banking as in manufacturing. Smaller community banks may be enjoying a differential value advantage, but may not be the market share leader. They may be employing a niche strategy, focusing on a smaller targeted segment than their larger counterparts. Such a focus may allow them to more closely provide the important value attributes demanded by their customers than can a larger bank. However, the benefits from reduced price elasticities and lower direct costs are definitely attainable.

How do these value effects combine to impact overall firm profitability? While this is a relatively new area of inquiry, some initial evidence is in. A study by Anderson, Fornell, and Lehmann of the relationship between value and profitability in Sweden concluded that "an annual one-point increase in customer satisfaction (defined in the study as value) has a net present value of $7.48 million over five years for a typical firm in Sweden. Given the sample's average net income of $65 million, this represents a cumulative increase of 11.5 percent." They further conclude "If the impact of customer satisfaction (value) on profitability is similar for firms in the *Business Week* 1000, then an annual one-point increase in the average firm's satisfaction index would be worth $94 million or 11.4 percent of current ROI."[9]

Closer to home is the case of Progressive Corporation, the auto insurer discussed earlier. How have efforts to increase the delivery of customer value impacted their performance? Progressive's net income of $267 million for 1993 has increased since 1989 (the year of the introduction of its new Immediate Response program) at an annual compound rate of 20 percent.[10]

Hampton Inns provides another example of how value translates into greater performance. Hampton Inns offers refunds to their customers if they are not satisfied with their stay, regardless of the reason. This policy generated $1.1 million in refunds during 1993. But the heightened customer value produced by the policy translated into an estimated $11 million in increased revenues.[11]

Lands' End, the giant mail order catalog company, also shows how a value strategy can produce significant performance impacts. The 1993 price of Lands' End men's twill pants is lower than the price they were charging in 1992. Their catalog explains this price change. "At $31 we thought last year's Popular Twills were a darned good value. Unfortunately for us, the boss didn't agree. '$31 is a good price but not a great price,' he bellowed. So we rolled up our sleeves. And after several gallons of coffee (and a few broken pencils), we came up with a lower price that would still allow us to keep our jobs: $29.50." With this kind of value focus applied throughout their operations it's not hard to understand how sales increased from $336.3 million in 1992 to about $400 million in 1993.[12] Value pays.

Value Proposition 5: What constitutes value today, will not necessarily define value tomorrow.

Sic transit valere mundi (like its counterpart glory, all value in this world is fleeting) must be the watchword for the bank implementing a customer value strategy. All value is indeed fleeting. To understand this proposition we need only recall the changes in the share of the financial asset market cited in Chapter 1. The value migration that has bled the commercial banking industry of its share of assets has been driven by customers redefining value and seeking this new value elsewhere.

No business or industry is immune from the transience of customer value. The American automobile industry failed to properly identify and understand what customers valued and suffered heavily from its own value myopia. Kmart can also attest to the transience of customer value as can IBM, Wang, and any number of other businesses that have failed to maintain a value vigilance. This is the lesson that we learn from history. Resources will flow to their greatest value. Failure to continually monitor what customers value, and your ability to continually satisfy this value need will prove costly.

Value Proposition 6: The bank that can identify, create, and maintain a differential value advantage will be less vulnerable to competitive pressures.

There is probably no better defense against competition than having customers who acknowledge that they cannot get better value elsewhere. Building a value fence around your customers means that any customer acquisition efforts targeted to your own customers will be extremely expensive and perhaps prohibitive.

With the emphasis on customer retention and the resulting profit potential that is associated with a successful retention effort, providing your customers with the best value in the business only makes sense. Remember, a dissatisfied bank customer can take, on average, a $23,000 deposit and a three product relationship with them when they leave in search of better value. Providing them with the best value possible will put a stop to these defections and allow you to build even more profitable relationships.

Customers are an asset that unfortunately does not show up explicitly on the bank's balance sheet. Think for a moment of the amount of investment your bank has made in attracting and keeping customers. Think also of the loss of financial market share that has plagued the commercial banking industry that we documented in Chapter 1, and ask how reinjecting value into the industry, one bank at a time and one product/market at a time, can arrest this loss of share and resulting loss of jobs and banks.

SOME CONCLUDING THOUGHTS

Value is an extremely potent concept when applied to an industry such as commercial banking. Understanding its properties and the various propositions attendant to it are crucial for the successful implementation of a philosophy of business based on value.

Value is perceptual in nature and is defined by the customer. Customers learn about value through experience which means that any bank has a direct impact on the value lessons it teaches its customers. There is also a portion of the value judgment that is not under the direct control of the bank. Customers learn about value from their friends and acquaintances.

There are six propositions concerning value. Understanding these propositions eases the implementation and strategic use of value as a competitive weapon. Finally, we have examined the linkage between a differential value advantage and profitability. In Chapter 7 we will provide empirical evidence of this relationship.

Endnotes

1. Davidson, William A. and Bro Uttal (1989) "Coming: The Customer Service Decade," *Across the Board*, November, p. 35.

2. Mena, Alberto (1994) "CDs That Try a Little Harder," *Business Week* (September 5), p. 90.

3. Henkoff, Ronald (1994) "Service is Everybody's Business," *Fortune* (June 27), p. 50.

4. Henkoff, p. 50.

5. Heskett, James L., Thomas O. Jones, George W. Loveman, W. Earl Sasser, and Leonard A. Schlesinger (1994) "Putting the Service-Profit Chain to Work," *Harvard Business Review* (March–April), p. 164.

6. Heskett, *et al.*

7. A conversation with Frank Meeks at the University of Southern Mississippi.

8. Grubbs, Ray and R. Eric Reidenbach (1991) *The Customer Service Renaissance; Lessons From the Banking Wars*, Chicago: Probus, p. 25.

9. Gale, Bradley T. (1994) *Managing Customer Value*, New York: The Free Press, p. 306.

10. Anderson, Eugene W., Claues Fornell, and Donald R. Lehman (1994) "Customer Satisfaction, Marker Share, and Profitability: Findings From Sweden," *Journal of Marketing*, Vol. 58 (July), p. 63.

11. Henkoff, p. 52.

12. Griesing, David (1994) "Quality: How to Make it Pay," *Business Week*, (August 8), pp. 56–57.

13. Caminiti, Susan (1989) "A Mail-Order Romance: Lands' End Courts Unseen Customers," *Fortune* (March 13), pp. 44–45.

3. The Value Philosophy Paradigm

> "Now, *here*, you see,
> it takes all the running
> you can do to keep in the
> same place. If you want
> to get somewhere else,
> you must run at least
> twice as fast as that."
> -*Through the Looking Glass*

It is no longer a simple world. Perhaps no one understands this more than a banker. There is no doubt that the world of financial services continues to change at a torrid pace. Given that pace, do established mental models adequately and relevantly describe present realities, or do they reflect an obsolescent world? Very few organizations in any industry have been able to keep pace with the effects of the technology explosion, deregulation, and globalization. Even when new technology is assimilated into an organization, there is a Doppler type effect that ripples throughout the organization like the ripples from a stone thrown into a quiet pond. Unfortunately, it doesn't mean the employees or the organization affected by the technology will make optimal use of the innovation.

Each bank manager interprets and lives the same operating reality differently. And, as we have pointed out earlier, this changing operating reality confronting commercial banking demands a new business philosophy. That philosophy, in turn, requires a new system paradigm, one that is more congruent with current operating realities than its predecessors, the production and sales philosophies.

We use the phrase "system paradigm" for several reasons. First, as in all systems, there exists an interrelationship among component parts that makes the system function. The proper *alignment* of these linkages is critical to the optimal operation of the system. Secondly, we can model this system, as well as the components and processes that make it operate. This is the paradigm. The system paradigm briefly explained in this chapter provides a baseline for discussion of some of the more critical components and processes.

THE NEW PARADIGM

The paradigm we are offering is a new conceptual apparatus that affects every aspect of the organization. Figure 3-1 is a depiction of the paradigm that begins with the Value Vision, that is the basis for a mission statement and articulation of the cultural components of the organization. Mission and culture effectively filter the subsystems of opportunities and the organizational structure. Opportunities contain the elements of environment and customers. Organization contains the elements of employees, innovation, and networks. Upon alignment of the subsystems and components, only then is it possible to produce the customer value that is the precursor of optimum profits.

It is nearly impossible to count the number of times we have seen companies change a strategy, adopt a new mission or attempt to exploit a new opportunity. They put all the new strategy in place, but do not change an element such as the compensation system, and then blame the new strategy for being inappropriate. It is analogous to changing the engine in a car, using the spark plugs from the old engine, and then wondering why the new engine doesn't run smoothly. The lesson we learn here is that all of the organizational systems and processes must align and interlock to attain optimal results. Failure to align the essential components of the paradigm results not in the reaching of the desired destination, but rather becoming lost in the maze of market forces and organizational pitfalls.

Figure 3-1
VALUE PARADIGM

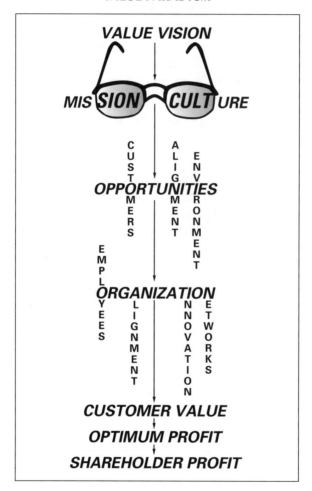

Focus on the customer value creating process outlined in this book is a method of fully capitalizing on opportunities and reaching the desired destination—optimal profitability. A new paradigm also means new evaluation criteria that are quite different from those used in the past. Today's customers only become a partner with organizations that deliver quality products and services, are organized to meet the customer's needs, and inspire the confidence necessary for any successful exchange relationship. This is a relationship or partnership where, in the long run, customer value and shareholder value converge. The critical components of this new paradigm are the organizational vision, mission, and culture—what we call the *value infrastructure* that could also be referred to generally as defining the purpose of the organization. Opportunities, sourced from both environmental trends and from customers, and the organization itself are the subcomponents that include the processes and people issues of the value creation process.

VISION/MISSION/CULTURE

Decisions regarding a bank's vision, mission, and culture are inextricably intertwined. Vision tells why the organization exists. Mission tells what the organization does in support of that vision. Culture is the pattern of beliefs and values that support both the vision and the mission, but at the same time are an important element that gives rise to the vision in the first place. Without *coherent entanglement* within this infrastructure, no organization can hope to compete on a value basis. This infrastructure is so important to the implementation of a value philosophy that we dedicate Chapter 4 to the topic.

Vision and mission spring from, and are the product of, the business philosophy of the bank. If it is a sales philosophy, then its vision, mission, and culture will reflect the different assumptions inherent in the sales philosophy. Likewise, if it is a value philosophy, the vision, mission, and culture of the bank will be shaped by the nature of the assumptions that are embedded within this philosophic orientation. If a philosophic orientation is obsolete or, if it does not truly reflect the operating reality of the bank, then the goal of optimum profitability will not be reached. Rather, the bank will end up in some operational cul-de-sac, losing valuable competitive momentum and organizational energy.

Philosophy, other than for a start-up firm, is historically based and, is a reflection of the cumulative values that are imbedded within the corporation. These values include elements such as ethics, people orientation, work environment, performance, and growth, as well as more current issues such as green management to preserve the earthly environment, diversity, multiculturalism, and social justice. To the extent that the bank's values are congruent with the market's values, the enterprise will have a greater chance for success.

It takes a conscious, objective effort to define and change an obsolete philosophy. Just ask General Motors or Xerox, a couple of the companies noted in Chapter 9 on continuous improvement. The adoption of a new business philosophy requires a new vision, a new supporting and congruent mission, and of equal importance, a modified, supportive culture. In short, a new philosophy requires a new infrastructure that will hold together the critical components of the new system paradigm. For many banks, the failure of the implementation of a sales philosophy or a customer service philosophy can be directly attributable to the absence of a supportive infrastructure. In many cases, banks have tried to adopt new business philosophies without changing old and obsolete infrastructures. Such adaptive efforts are doomed to failure, unless the considerable efforts to change are made. A number of adaptive considerations are discussed in Chapter 10.

This change effort is especially important when an organization has successfully lived a historical paradigm for many years. Kmart, for example, has not been able to change their paradigm in spite of a seemingly well-crafted vision and mission, while Wal-mart, in the spirit of its founder Sam Walton, has been able to capitalize on Kmart's lack of follow-through. Many banks have a similar history of evolving philosophies and a similarly bleak future unless they can adapt to new paradigms compatible with existing operating realities. No doubt you have witnessed first-hand the discomfort, fear, and frustration associated with a changing business philosophy. Too often the adoption of new philosophies is not successfully implemented. Typically, this can be explained by the failure to develop a new infrastructure, one that is compatible with and supportive of the new philosophy.

OPPORTUNITIES

Corporate opportunity assessments can be depicted as an organizational product/market matrix as explained in detail in Chapter 5. These corporate or SBU (Strategic Business Unit) level matrices provide direction for the opportunities that will be pursued by the organization, both present and future. Opportunities are sourced from the mission and business philosophy of the organization. For example, a firm such as Ben & Jerry's Ice Cream would likely be involved in opportunities flavored with social responsibility because they claim that as part of their vision and mission.

But opportunities for a line manager are much more specific than global corporate opportunities. Manager opportunities deal with specific product/markets, segments within those product/markets, and the organizational initiatives that are chosen within those arenas. Corporate business philosophy is the basis for specification of the services and markets in which a bank chooses to compete (The terms product and service are interchangeable for purposes of this discussion.) When these services and markets are placed in the context of a matrix it becomes apparent that opportunities can be prioritized for the bank, and the methodology to do so is explained in Chapter 5. This prioritization is driven directly from the organizational infrastructure. Two major sources of opportunity for financial service institutions are its operating environment and customers.

Environment

A principal opportunity source is found in the interplay of various components of the bank's operating environment. These environmental components include technology, competition, the cultural and social fabric of a global market system, the economy, the legal/political/regulatory environment, and resource supply.

Current emphasis on technology and competition is a reflection of their greater short-term impact. Changes in regulation, such as interstate banking laws or the DIDMCA of 1980, have also unleashed many opportunities for the bank poised to take advantage of them.

Many banks have found significant opportunity to better provide and receive greater customer service at lower costs by outsourcing various banking functions. Establishing these relationships to deliver increased customer value requires the insight to identify where value opportunities exist. Again, at the expense of belaboring a point, the value infrastructure provides focus and clarity to the identification of environmental opportunities.

There are numerous value opportunities embedded within the various social changes taking place. Globalization, the influx of minorities into the workforce, the graying of America, and multiculturalism and diversity all represent social changes that, for the bank capable and willing to respond, are laden with value creating opportunities. One bank that has capitalized on such opportunities is Citibank. The traumatic grapple with bad loans in the United States notwithstanding, Citibank has taken the technology base for consumer products and exported it to the international arena. In countries from Europe to Asia, Citibank has introduced services that include consumer credit, telephone banking, 24-hour teller machines, and credit cards. An additional benefit to Citibank, which capitalizes on the global increase in tourism, is that traveling customers have been more than pleased with the international access to funds. Citibank's international business has been growing at a healthy and profitable pace.

Customers

Customers are a critical part of the bank's operating reality. Customers have to be co-producers or co-designers of the very production system itself. This means producers and consumers have to *know* a great deal about each other. A bank must perceive itself as a *knowledge system*, no longer as simply a factory for transforming material inputs to material outputs.

One often overlooked or prematurely rejected issue is the study of noncustomers. Why aren't they your customers? Why are they loyal and how loyal are they to competitive offerings? What determines whether they would switch institutions? Another key failing of banks that do not excel in providing valued service is the tendency to view their customer base as one big, universal account. Customer groups have very different choice criteria. *Knowing* these choice criteria is essential to producing strong customer relationships. An innovative idea in this regard is offered by Dell Computer. Dell Computer has created a service capability based on the requirement that customers must be *pleased*, not just *satisfied*.[1] Being pleased is a result of the value gained from a transaction, whereas satisfaction is simply a form of passive acceptance. As discussed throughout this book, optimum profitability only follows the satisfaction of customer needs that have identifiable value to the customer.

ORGANIZATION

A third subsystem of the paradigm is collectively referred to as organization. Within the area of organization we emphasize such important subcomponents and processes as employees, performance standards, innovation, and networks. Any of these subcomponents and processes can lead to the creation of value that provides an organization with the differentiation necessary for a sustainable market advantage. This value differentiation is useful, however, only when it relates to value as perceived by the customer, and only when the value is perceived by the customer as sourced from an aligned organization will that value produce optimum profits.

Instilling a continuous learning culture in the organization produces the fluidity required to adapt quickly and take advantage of marketplace opportunities.[2] Fewer ready-made market gaps or needs exist today relative to just five years ago. It is necessary, at the very least, to understand the customer's value creating process and to match offerings to it in a variety of creative ways. This matching is a creative process that is nearly impossible without an attitude of continuous improvement that is explained in Chapter 9.

Whatever the organizational environment a manager inherits, shaping or reshaping it is critically important. Two major elements dictate work environment: (1) the business philosophy that defines what the company is like and how it operates, and (2) how the people on the front line live the philosophical concepts and values that prevail to define what it's like to work there. Reflective performance standards set the quality and pace of people's efforts.

How many review sessions in your bank actually reject long-winded diatribes, poorly prepared plans with bogus or wishful profit targets? Acceptance of such plans, complaints notwithstanding, is really a denial of reality. Instead of complaining about these places and ultimately accepting them, managers wanting to instill the responsibility and creativity necessary to adopt a value philosophy will find a way to allow themselves, as well as other employees, the flexibility necessary to pursue that philosophy. Goals and objectives, reviewed in sessions that acknowledge and accept responsibility and allow creativity are different. They are a risk-laden prediction of potential accomplishments for the next week or month or quarter. In the absence of those session attributes, there is a reinforcement of the belief that the future will be no different from the past. The alternative is to take responsibility and assure that the future will, in fact, be different.

Employees

Employee considerations involve things such as employee selection, training, teamwork, commitment to the vision, and retention. Money is important, but it is even more important that employees enjoy what they do and are really excited about it. Motivation is the result of commitment, and leadership becomes a modeling activity for that commitment. Modeling here refers to acting the part and having others follow suit. Modeling behavior implies that employees must be intertwined with customers, and thereby a part of the identification of value opportunities catalyzes the creativity and innovative learning behavior necessary to adapt to an ever-changing environment. Employees are an integral part of efforts to bring value to the customer through higher levels of service and best cost production. Examples of identifying employee integration are contained in the chapter on designing a value-added delivery system.

Performance Standards and Measures

Performance standards are most important as a determinant of the quality and pace of effort your bank puts out. Perhaps no where is the concept of alignment more critical than the linkage between value and performance. The single biggest contribution you can make to immediate results and long-term success is to raise performance expectations for every manager and employee, not just for yourself. Deployment of resources for long-term advantage is often dependent on the validity and reliability of the performance measures. Our experience shows that the issue of reliability of measurement is often addressed, but once the measure has been established its validity is seldom questioned. Time can invalidate a measure in the same way it can invalidate a philosophic orientation. Standards are just one piece of a much larger puzzle, however, and as with any single piece it is unwise to focus on it alone. Chapter 6 examines in greater detail the concept of strategic value measurement.

Innovation

Innovation is fundamental to business success in the dynamic and highly competitive financial services sector, and is the *raison d'être* for continuous improvement as an organizational attribute. Rapidly changing information technology, new customer needs, deregulation, and increasing competitive threats are a few reasons it is a cornerstone. As we delineate in Chapter 9, innovation is not a quick fix, and using it as a quick fix will lead to disillusionment.

One example of a bank that was an innovator in fee-earning activities and has taken the lead in the information business is State

Street Boston Corp. Wall Street analysts have not always agreed with that organization's investments, but it has consistently produced returns based on an innovative approach to the business. It is an example of how financial institutions must prioritize more carefully than they have in the past and allocate resources to truly meritorious projects.[3] The world of financial services is very different from even a decade ago—ATMs, smart cards, on-line information, economic development incentives, investment management, and the promised advent of cybercash are a few examples. As is evident from these examples, not only can stagnation be a sign of crisis, but so too is rapid change. Rapid growth, although seldom perceived as such, is a another sure sign of crisis among those who are unprepared.

Networks

Networks, sometimes referred to in the literature as strategic alliances, involve items such as acquisitions, mergers, supplier and customer partnerships, and outsourcing. Networks have become an increasingly important element as the global interdependence of the banking system has increased and regulatory issues have evolved. Networks essentially provide the flexibility to address variant opportunities, especially when those opportunities require resources that could provide a higher return elsewhere, require investment that would render the opportunity noncompetitive, or require investments beyond the scope of current resources.

Networking is fundamentally a creative process addressing interconnecting arrangements. It has such advantages as capitalizing on technology transfers and process expertise, surmounting otherwise formidable barriers to entry, start-up costs, R&D, and patent rights. An example of gaining a differential advantage with a cost-savings partnership that creates customer value is a Wal-mart deal with Fisher Price to produce specific toys exclusively for distribution by Wal-mart that embody value for Wal-mart customers.

ALIGNMENT

Various elements of the value paradigm are explained in the following chapters of this book. The single most important issue in explicating the paradigm is the absolute necessity for congruent linkages among the elements. If the vision is not supported by the mission and linked coherently to the opportunities, things just don't happen for the bank. With purposeful linkages established at the top of the paradigm, it is then necessary to align the elements within the domains of opportunity and organization. Aligning technology (e.g., ATMs), employees (e.g., compensation), and networks (e.g., supplier partnership) are necessary to produce the most profit attainable by the bank. If, and only if, such an alignment exists is your bank in a position to create a sustainable differential value advantage that meets customer needs and produces the greatest profits. Note that alignment of a single item, for example, customer satisfaction or any of the other elements, can produce increased bottom line, but until all elements are aligned the organization is foregoing the value associated with the other elements.

The biggest change in conventional production or sales-oriented organizations is that alignment requires the organization to become a learning organization. The people and the processes must continually readjust to maintain the value differentiation in a sustained form, and one key to building front-line confidence is a greater investment in people. Training must be viewed as an investment, not an expense. If your bank is not willing to invest in its people, how can your institution expect to change? An often quoted saying from Eastern philosophy is "Insanity is defined as doing the same thing and expecting different results!"

An example from a recently published study on small community banks reveals how important alignment is.[4] For example, inadequate training can lead to incompetent employees that in turn lead to more time required for implementation. The nonalignment of necessary training produces a nearly overwhelming issue for the community bank. Problems of alignment occur in both large and small organizations, but smaller banks are more likely to experience the adverse effects of misalignment because when several problems occur simultaneously they have a greater impact on the smaller bank.

VALUE

Elements of the paradigm are driving forces that stimulate the creation of value. Stimulation of new business due to greater value being offered in today's economy is through a greater density of resources available to the individual user. Density here refers to activities per unit of space and time.[5] Space and time are ever more valuable commodities to individuals based on trends such as dual career families, single heads of household, and globalized opportunities. More value is created as networks are developed and mobilized. Customers are regarded as participants in the co-production of value, and are encouraged to adopt this role rather than remaining passive.

Price and value are generally considered to go hand-in-hand. Price is commonly driven, however, by production costs, input prices, and other cost-related measures consistent with accounting techniques left over from historical orientations. For financial institutions, when the cost of borrowing money is the basis for lending, there is no indication of the value to the borrower. The value that is placed on the customer offering by the organization is thus based on historical conditions, in a kind of rear-view mirror perspective. If we consider the value that the offering has to customers today as the basis for pricing, the situation can change drastically. In order to have value-laden offerings, a financial institution must have detailed knowledge about customers and their value-perceiving processes. For example, if customers are primarily interested in new *solutions that would produce value by making more services available per unit of time*, it will be of virtually no interest to them that the bank succeeds in cutting costs and lowering the price of the inputs. Customer value would accrue to such things as automatically moving money to the highest interest-bearing account or one visit mortgage handling. If activities are perceived as valuable only by the bank and not by the customer, competition has relatively easy access to the customer willing to pay begrudgingly on a one-time basis.

Currently, the strongest force working against a value orientation is the short-term expectations imposed by pressure on the selling function to maximize profit without consideration of strategic health.

In any situation where creativity is sought, the beginning point is customer needs. An example from several years ago involves a product now known as the Mailmobile that was developed by Lear-Siegler Inc. The profit margin according to industry standards would have been about $1,500 per unit. Upon studying the needs of the customers and positioning the product to align more closely with their needs, the margin was about $15,000. A zero here and a zero there and pretty soon you are talking about some real money!

Another example of value being more than just price is from AT&T's regional sales force. Their equation is: Value = Quality + Reliability + Innovation + Service + Price. They use the acronym QRISP when referring to the equation, and it certainly says price is only a part of the equation. They act the message as well as talk about it through the Maximum Advantage program that ensures a customer that he or she will be placed into the plan that is most cost-effective, and a credit will be issued if AT&T fails to do so.

An example of value from financial services is the All-In-One or Asset Management accounts. These accounts combine checking, credit/debit cards, and brokerage services. Any available cash is automatically swept into a money market account to prevent loss of interest between transactions. Prudent money management says this service is worth something to the customer, whether as a fee for service or as loyalty to the institution. It is also worth noting that the service was pioneered by Merrill Lynch, not by a bank.

Many banks tried to imitate this service without real consideration of the value needed by their customers. In so doing, a large number of these "me-too" banks invested significant amounts of time, effort, and cash into a service that their customers did not value. The returns from these misadventures verify the lack of value.

We inhabit a very different world from the textbooks. Customers and suppliers need to stay together in durable relationships, protracted networks, and mutual commitments extended over many years. Costs of selling products to customers who do not really value them are too high and, ultimately, we outwit ourselves by designing and selling such products. Value is the product of mutual concern and painstaking cooperation. This isn't magic stuff, and a perpetual search for a stargate hidden in the maze is both futile and costly. Our proposition is just good sound business practice and systems logic.

Demands for a change in paradigm are simultaneously exciting and disturbing. Value inheres and accumulates in the complex web of relationships between suppliers and customers. Value is mutually constructed by partners that form clusters composed of many value-added chains, a mutualism of value co-created by a dialogue of partners, if you will. Fewer customers wish to be the passive recipients of something prepackaged for them by a supplier who claims to know exactly what they want before meeting them. Unilateral selling propositions with the purpose of manipulation of the other and in order to sell a bill of goods is history. Strategic marketing investment for the creation of customer value is the key to continuous profitability.

WATCH OUT FOR FADS

A plethora of fads are often touted as new conceptual approaches to enhance efficiencies and profits. Recent ones include TQM, streamlining, downsizing, right-sizing, empowerment, customer focus, and reengineering. Of these, only reengineering holds out a promise of sufficiently restructuring an organization to meet the inexorable demands of today's markets. The evidence and experience we have indicates a reengineering toward creation of customer value is a key ingredient for success in the world of financial problem solving. Each of the other techniques can help a bank do what it already does less expensively or more productively, but cannot alone provide the sustainable advantage of a systems perspective of the business. In the face of a changing operating reality, doing what you are currently doing, even less expensively or more productively, "...takes all the running you can do to keep in the same place." You go nowhere. An example of following one doctrine at the expense of others is Florida Power & Light chasing the Baldridge Quality award and losing money in the pursuit. Most of these techniques dwell on today rather than tomorrow. Adhere to the words of Wayne Gretzky when asked why he was so great, "I'm great because I skate to where the puck will be, not where it is." Creating customer value is where the puck will be.

SUMMARY

Banks interested in long-term success recognize that the world is changing rapidly, and mere change within structures and processes to fit today's crisis does not insure a win in the competitive battles of the twenty-first century. Longer-term questions are usually tougher and more vague, and vision is a long-term question. Focus on fix-it type solutions has many times led to bloated organizational structures and processes, a loss of focus, and a view from the rear-view mirror rather than the windshield. The first step must be to decide where you are going as an articulated vision, and then allow the details of how to get there be placed behind that vision to support it.

Endnotes

1. Nonaka, Ikujiro. (1991) "The Knowledge Creating Company," *Harvard Business Review*, (November–December), pp. 96–104.

2. Garvin, David A. (1993) "Building A Learning Organization." *Harvard Business Review*, (July–August), pp. 78–91.

3. Cooper, Robert G. *et al.* (1994) "What Distinguishes the Top Performing New Products in Financial Services?" *Journal of Product Innovation and Management*, Vol. 11, No. 4, (September), pp. 281–299.

4. Kargar, Javad and Robert A. Blumenthal. (1994) "Successful Implementation of Strategic Decisions in Small Community Banks," *Journal of Small Business Management*, (April), pp. 10–22.

5. Drucker, Peter F. (1994) "The New Productivity Challenge," *Harvard Business Review*, (November–December), pp. 69–79.

4. Developing the Value Infrastructure

T he value paradigm is a view of organizational modernity that banks are yet to discover. The complex interplay among vision, mission, and culture forms what we call the value infrastructure. It is this infrastructure that will energize, direct, and support the bank's efforts at creating the all important differential value advantage. Common to all well-run organizations is a shared vision of what that organization needs to be. This vision helps the organization identify the critical business arenas that define its mission. In conjunction with this mission is the cultural values of the organization. Taken together, they provide the value infrastructure upon which all customer value creation depends. Without this value infrastructure, attempts to compete in the value arena are futile. This chapter will examine what we consider to be the critical factors of this value infrastructure beginning with vision.

VISION

For today's banking industry, the question is not whether to cultivate a vision. Every bank has one whether it recognizes its official existence or not. Rather, the issue facing banks is what *priority* its leaders are assigning to the vision, and how it should best be *managed* in order to *shape* the future of the bank.

The most fundamental choice any human being can make is to create a future of their own choosing. That is precisely the dilemma confronting the commercial banking industry: To create its own future or ride, rudderless and without direction, the currents of a constantly changing operating reality. In Western society we believe strongly in freedom of choice, the choice not to be dependent and be controlled by someone else's choices. It is pervasive in the fundamental arguments for free enterprise. And yet, either unwittingly or perhaps fearfully we sometimes abdicate the responsibility inherent in freedom of choice by allowing other's decisions to lead the way. Ironically, we are using our freedom of choice to give up freedom! Such was the warning voiced by Joseph Schumpeter over 50 years ago.[1]

More than once, as consultants, we have seen how one organization's apparent vision has been dictated by another, more far-sighted organization. Corporate America's quality vision of the 1970s and 1980s, such that it was, was the carefully crafted product of Japan's well-articulated vision of quality. Creating a vision of our own choosing for ourselves and our organizations is incumbent on every one of us as responsible members of free society and of the various organizations to which we belong. Understanding the context and value of a vision and how it links ultimately to the creation of a sustainable value advantage through mission, culture, and communication efforts is addressed in this chapter.

The term "vision" is often misunderstood and perhaps even more often misused. There seem to be as many definitions of the term as there are articles on the subject. Organizational vision is not a new concept. It is the reincarnation of a credo or corporate values statement or guiding principles. Each of these were attempts to articulate the culture of an organization. To clarify the use of the term is to ask the question, "Do employees in my bank have a *clear and shared understanding* of the future?" Do they understand "What kind of financial services institution we need to be ten years from now?" Can they answer the question "What opportunities for creating and delivering customer value will provide us with the basis for enjoying a sustainable differential value advantage?"

Too often there is excessive energy devoted to preserving the past and not enough energy to creating the future. Many banks have too little vision and do not clearly articulate why they exist. Such is the problem facing many banks lacking in vision as they struggle to survive the day-to-day tactical demands imposed by regulators. It is understandable how vision about customer value can be relegated to the more "important and pressing" demands of Regulation DD, CRA, or RESPA.

Others who have articulated the vision have not communicated it throughout the organization. Some become encumbered with a vision statement that is pages long and confuses mission, company values, philosophy, objectives, strategies, Short-term issues, and may even contain a couple of well chosen paragraphs from their new CD-ROM training disc. Such an approach occludes rather than gives context to the future. One author calls this the "Vision Trap."[2]

Simply stated, a vision, whether at a corporate level or a unit within an organization, is putting into words the future you desire for your bank. An effective vision is concise and clear. It is understood by everyone in the bank, providing guidance for why the bank exists. It is the quintessential act of leadership, the modeling by senior management for every employee in the bank. The top person in a bank, the place where the buck stops, must be the source of the corporate vision for the bank. General managers must consistently influence the basic business concepts the institution adopts. It is clear from experiences with many organizations that assembling a team to develop a consensual vision statement is like asking the Cheshire Cat to run the dog pound. It just doesn't work very well. In mature organizations the mission may be inherited from predecessors, but the top person is still responsible for ascribing to a vision and supporting it with every decision.

An example of vision is evident in the history of Ted Turner's CNN news network. Turner had a vision of a 24-hour news network to rival the unassailed big three network news organizations. He took that vision to a group of his executives, hired people that could live the message, and took the tremendous risks inherent in any such venture of greatness.[3]

Closer to home is the vision articulated by Luke Helms, former CEO of Seafirst Bank in Seattle and currently an executive with Bank of America. Helms saw the future of his banking system operated as a McDonald's. Each branch is a franchise run and owned by employees. Corporate headquarters exists to provide operational support, advertising, and product development. This vision articulates a preferred state, a destination, and contains within it a guiding philosophy.

A vision is meant to guide the bank into a preferred future, a desirable, ideal state. It is an expression of optimism. It is not an easy task to articulate, and more than a few people have struggled with the task. An effective vision statement is generally:

1. **Brief**—It is comprised of a couple of sentences that people can remember and put into effect daily.

2. **A Guiding Philosophy**—It articulates why the organization exists.

3. **Sets High Sights**—There is a long-term thrust, a destination to strive for. It leads on and on and is not necessarily achievable in concrete terms.

It is important to realize here that it is the job of every manager, not just the CEO, to have a vision. The belief that leadership and vision lies in the hands of others and that the future is for others to decide is essentially an abdication of control leading to victimization and a setup to blame others. A well-articulated and communicated vision allows us to stay away from the dangerous unknown that is rife with unpredictability and (mostly imagined) danger.

A top-down order falsely protects us in a variety of ways. The implicit patriarchal contract historically espoused by most large organizations is no longer a safe haven, if it ever was. This is evidenced by the restructuring and large scale separations in the Fortune 50 during the 1990s, as well as the significant job loss in the banking industry that we discussed earlier. Taking a stand that is in your own best interest and advocating a position you believe in is risky, but it's free.

"I don't like belonging to another person's dream."
-Alice in *Through the Looking Glass.*

Do you?

Several aspects of taking the risk of specifying a vision are important. First, there is an implicit statement that things could be better than they are now, and therefore past decisions might have been better or might even have been wrong. Second guessing on the part of those unwilling or unable to take a stand can be expected. Second, the vision will possibly, and quite likely, be in conflict with visions of others. Conflict does not mean that there is no congruence, nor does it mean that there aren't pieces of the vision that could be improved through interaction. However, to be effective as a guiding philosophy, the vision must be shared. Third, specification has an implicit accountability attached. Living by the rules we create for ourselves is more difficult than living by other's rules. We can justify breaking other's rules, but it's much more difficult to justify breaking our own.

What distinguishes a meaningless generality from a useful vision is the grounded reality of (un)supported assumptions and (wishful) thinking about comparative performance. It is difficult today to write about vision, mission, or strategy without talking about giving customers better value than your competitors do. Yet talking about the concept and integrating it with daily activities are two different things. Value creation in a learning organization will drive a bank toward a continuous value improvement cycle. Stated strategy is not always strategy as realized, and a good manager can distinguish between espoused theory and theory in use.[4]

Bill Gates of Microsoft Corp. has always been one to paint a lofty and expansive vision. It began with "A computer on every desk, in every office running Microsoft software," and has more recently been phrased as "Our software will be used in the home, in the pocket, and in the car."[5] When the PC was the future the first statement served the company well. With the proliferation of PCs and the advancement of technology, Gates has appropriately expanded the vision to include the information highway.

There is certainly no guarantee of success just because an appropriate vision exists. One of the on-line services Gates is developing is a full-service center (code named Marvel) for the information highway. Such a service could yet *expand* the potential of bank ATMs, which have already changed a significant value proposition of banking. It could also *diminish* the use of ATMs within certain market segments. The infrastructure for ATMs and charge cards will likely merge, thereby reconfiguring the buying power and transaction services required to be a player in the new financial services industry. This new infrastructure will provide value where users are demanding it: service time, location, prestige, and authorization speed.[6] Computers, software, communications, and merchant relationships will be changed as a result of the change in infrastructure. And the changes won't stop there. They will eventually affect the way all financial services are transacted from mortgages to stock purchases. Such a restructuring is more of an adventure in failure than a pathway to success, but the only pathway to success is through a vision. Those banks lacking in vision will, more than likely, be roadkill on the information highway.

Why Is Vision Important?

Five reasons why the specification of a shared vision is important are:

1. **Provides something worth risking for.** A way of discovering for employees that serving the bank also serves our self-interest. The very loftiness of the statement needs to capture the imagination and engage the spirit, giving the entire bank reason for spirited performance.

2. **Instills commitment.** Enrollment, affinity, compliance, or capitulation simply are not enough reasons. Instilling commitment and motivating the organization is a difficult and arduous task. Anything less than commitment, however, will be reflected in the results of the organization.[7]

3. **Permits alignment.** A shared vision guides the congruent and coherent linkage of each process and each activity to the importance of making the bank successful. A well defined vision is a necessary condition for beginning creation of aligned teamwork toward the attainment of optimum profits.

4. **Becomes an anchor for consistency.** A commonly contributing factor to mediocre performance is a lack of consistency rather than effort or enthusiasm. A written vision provides an anchor point for consistency.

5. **Requires accountability.** Passing the buck and blaming others is in vogue today. To take a stand or not is an expression of our own personal values. Committing to something that matters and accepting responsibility for it is the essence of freedom of choice. Most people see commitment as fraught with risks of being wrong. If you haven't been wrong lately, you haven't been trying!

Myths about Vision

There are a number of myths about vision that we have uncovered by working with companies that are successful and profitable.

1. **It's about being #1.** It seems that every television sports broadcast has someone with their index finger in the air. Being #1 is a mission or an objective, not a vision.

2. **Practical.** No, it's more empyreal than real. If we never step out toward the vision it will remain a dream. It's the dream that is the basis for the vision, and dreams are seldom practical.

3. **Begin with customers.** Currently the fad is to develop "customer focus." That focus can deny assumptions about: the environment, a variety of networking possibilities, and the emphasis required for a motivated work-force. Customers are only one element of the focus.

4. **Treat customers well and employees will take care of themselves.** This avoids the interdependence required to move toward the vision. Customers and employees are not separate entities. The broader view is that stakeholders are interdependent.

5. **It's a jungle.** No, just foliage. If the world is viewed as a dangerous, fearful place, striving for a dream doesn't make the list of things to do. Being able to assess and take risks is an important aspect of turning a dream into a vision that we work at every day.

6. **Commitment is enrollment, affinity, compliance, or capitulation.** Don't be self-deceived. Commitment is the only state that engenders the motivation necessary to realize a dream.

7. **Vision lives forever.** Eventually all business philosophies become obsolete, and the first reaction to obsolescence is invariably a defensive one. Changes over time must prompt questions such as: What kind of business do we want to run? Are we in the right fields? Do we still have a viable position in each? How should we be reshaping the business? How do we shift in small ways in a consistent

direction? In combination, such questions will indicate the relevance of the vision.

Crafting an Infrastructure

Ten steps, with due apologies to David Letterman, will help you craft an infrastructure that includes an aligned vision, mission, and culture.

1. **Clarify Your Motivations.** Many motives are subliminal, and focusing on these motives and the underlying assumptions will help to clarify and link the business realities. Personal issues and business issues are often intertwined here. Clarifying motivations early on makes the next nine steps easier.

2. **Audit Your Culture.** Assuming there is an ongoing business, what is the real orientation? Look naively at the business and the environment. The perspective from an organizational outsider will lend objectivity. Some contend that an inside perspective, or water cooler talk, is sufficient, but it doesn't maximize probability of discovering the reality, especially if the business has been around for a while. Many CEOs want to redefine the direction of their organization, but are frustrated in their attempts by an intransigent culture. Unspoken and unexamined assumptions, values, and myths often block an objective assessment of reality. There is a natural tendency to downplay uncomfortable realities.

3. **Articulate Your Vision.** What is the picture in your mind's eye? Not the public vision, the private one. As any writer can attest, the vision held in your own imagination is rearticulated many times. Attempts at communication to each person becomes an iterative process. An organizational vision that pushes every organizational member to perform their best in creating and delivering ultimate value to customers, that creates an environment where

everyone does their best work, and that is energizing is assisted with a concise and coherent articulation. Just look at the plethora of examples of threatened plant or store closings and the super efforts put forth in those circumstances. They are examples of an energized, shared vision.

4. **Define Your Business.** What are you doing and what do you want to be doing? What would it be like to expand your scale and scope?

5. **Modify Your Assumptions.** Assumptions are the roots identified in the culture audit in #2. Deadly opposition can arise within the organization when assumptions are identified that are perceived as encroaching on sacred ground. Vested interests turn out in force when they feel encroachment. Anticipate the reaction.

6. **Modify Models.** The CEO might say there is compassion but Captain Kickass gets the promotions. The words might be there but the models, processes, and systems still reflect outdated and inaccurate assumptions. Respect differences while modeling desired behavior. Help with modifying the models and their underlying dimensions.

7. **Modify Systems and Processes.** Considering modified assumptions, create the linkages necessary for aligned performance appraisals, compensation, and feedback systems. Without both alignment and accuracy within systems and processes, it's nearly impossible to affect change. University systems are great examples of espousing change but not aligning the systems and processes.

8. **Assist People.** Mistakes at the cutting edge of change are different and more risky than others, but also more valuable. In pioneering innovation necessary for change, the change agents need support and encouragement.

9. **Apply the Value Test.** Ask the questions and listen naively to the answers from the Introduction of this book. If you still have questions, call us!

10. Modify 3 – 8. Start Over. This is part and parcel of the continuous learning in Chapter 9. The feedback loop is automatic in a continuous learning environment, and superfluous in all others.

MISSION

What differentiates a bank's vision from its mission? A mission is a statement, emanating from the vision statement, of what business we are in and possibly what ranking we have or aspire to. A mission is attainable in some foreseeable future with a time limit and finish line. It becomes a challenging term goal that is attainable while incurring intelligent risk—a road map to drive the business. It provides the necessary guidance to formulate structure, processes, and daily activities that move us, as a financial service institution, a step closer to the vision. It is a challenge to people to reexamine what they take for granted, and hence provides a clearer sense of direction by helping everyone to understand what roads will take them toward the vision. It is the inculcation process that envisions the future, creating new concepts to meet it, and helping to implement those concepts in the real world. Missions need to intertwine customers, employees, suppliers, regulators, and the environment. These elements, combined with the knowledge necessary to be a learning organization are the bases for defining and adding value for each customer along the value chain as well as for the end user. In the absence of a vision, once a mission is accomplished, you lose sight of your next waypoint and are rudderless, no longer having direction. You're like Alice, not caring where you go as long as it's somewhere.

A necessary caution at this point has been heralded in the literature for the past three decades, that is, a tendency to be myopic when defining the business.[8] The classic example has been that railroads thought they were in the railroad business when they were really in the transportation business. Had they been more far-sighted they could conceivably still have a major share of the business rather than being a line for government subsidy.

At banking schools, workshops, and seminars this myopia is abundantly evident throughout the managerial ranks of bankers. When executives are asked "What does their bank do?" it is common to hear responses such as:

- We make loans.
- We sell checking accounts.
- We sell mutual funds.

These are functional definitions of what the bank does, and like the railroads, fails to incorporate a more strategic view of the industry. This is not only myopic, it is deadly.

A more far-sighted view or definition of the business might examine why the functions identified above are more or less valued by customers. People value checking accounts because they do not want to carry large amounts of cash with them. They value mortgage or auto loans because they can't afford the total price of a home or a car. These functions exist to solve peoples' financial service problems. Extending this reasoning to a more strategic plane would lead these executives to understand that their bank exists, and will continue to exist, only as long as their customers value the bank's financial problem-solving capabilities. And, as we have seen earlier, the value migration is on as customers are taking their business to competitors who are providing greater customer value. These competitors have a greater understanding of their niches in the financial services industry than do commercial banks.

As an example of the difficulty in attempting to define vision and mission statements, a heavy equipment dealer had the following mission statement espoused by the top management executive committee:

"(The Dealer) is in business to promote the sale of and provide product support services for heavy equipment and power systems products of (the manufacturer)."

The real business for the dealer is earth moving and power generation, not the above functional description of how the business makes money. Their justification of the statement was that it was a conscious decision that they felt comfortable with. The organization is quite well managed, has a proud history, has reasonably motivated employees, and they are producing a profit. The following questions would be relevant:

- Is the statement short term?
- Does it accurately define the industry in which they operate?
- Will it carry the company prosperously into the future?
- Does it motivate and energize the organization?
- Is there an emphasis on the future rather than the past?
- Does it network sufficiently with suppliers and customers?
- Is it so specific that it curtails innovation and selection of opportunities?
- Are the philosophic assumptions clear enough to resolve conflicts or are they resolved by some other means, such as charismatic leadership or line authority, or do they remain unresolved?

A key element underlying an effective mission statement is that the assumptions must fit reality. Assumptions about environment, mission, strengths and core competencies must fit with each other. For example, the orientation of the business, as discussed previously, must be known and understood throughout the organization. Each employee must understand the relationship between competitive advantage, value creation, and business strategy. The foundations of every manager's job: shaping the future work environment, setting strategy, allocating resources, developing managers, building the organizational future, and overseeing operations, must be aligned with the mission, and in turn with the vision—if optimum profitability is a possibility. Otherwise, the firm creates its own glass ceiling, is unable to erase old boundaries and draw new ones, and essentially creates a world that by definition continues to be more and more obsolete.

CULTURE

Culture refers to the values and beliefs that are rooted in a company and are a result of the orientation of the company. Culture has a far-reaching effect on attitudes and behavior and characterizes life in the organization. It exerts a behavior shaping influence on organizational members.

Most banks have been through massive cultural changes as operating realities have changed and forced banks to search for new business philosophies. In an earlier chapter we examined how several philosophies of business have, to a greater or lesser extent, shaped the beliefs, attitudes, assumptions, and behaviors of employees within banks. The production philosophy promoted an inside order taker culture. With the advent of a sales philosophy, the culture changed to support a more aggressive selling effort on the part of bank employees. As this philosophy of business gave way to the customer service philosophy, bank cultures again underwent a change. Now dominant values and attitudes were focused on the servicing of customers. Their wants and needs became the central focus of banking. As the operating reality of banking changes once again, bank cultures must to change to support those activities necessary to provide optimal customer value. The bank's vision and mission must not upside this cultural change but not drive it. The vision and mission must instill the key values, beliefs, attitudes, and behaviors necessary to respond to customers' demand for value.

In the mid-1980s, GTE Corporation distributed a booklet entitled *Vision * Values.* Contained therein were seven values claimed critical to GTE's long-term success. Those values were: quality, benchmarking, employee involvement and teamwork, people, innovation, technology, and market sensitivity. These values were meant to guide daily work activities and instill dedication to employees, customers, ethical standards, shareholder expectations, and social responsibility. They were an attempt on the part of GTE to articulate the values underlying GTE's corporate culture. Few banks have ever taken such a bold step.

Some cultural issues are taken for granted and people are hardly aware of them. Others are more conscious and articulated. In any organization there is generally one predominant view of customer value, which can thus be said to be part of the culture. If management believes that the relevant value for success and survival is already available to the customer, then there will be little interest in adding new value and little new value will be forthcoming. But, if it is felt that current value is improvable, then the right mindset exists for stepping up value production and scanning appropriate new value opportunities from the outside.

Emerson Electric Co. is an example of a company that constantly added value by cutting costs. The vision of Chuck Knight, Chairman and CEO, was to be the "best cost producer." That vision has recently been modified to be "best cost producer with growth." Knight has been imminently successful thus far, and he has recreated a focused mindset that could again bode well for the future of Emerson. He has developed a culture that even he admits is somewhat myopic, but in spite of that myopia has the flexibility to accommodate a tectonically changing environment. It added value for the customer by cutting internal cost, and that was certainly appropriate for Emerson's basic industrial type products. Everyone in the company is aware of the culture and the recent redefinition of focus and is motivated by that focus.[9]

It's easy to end up with cultural conflicts—just don't say what's important to you. Vision drives the culture, and a manager must develop a vision for the business and oversee any necessary change in culture to accomplish it. This type of strategic thinking is a creative process that involves identifying possibilities, not simply evaluating known options. Such strategic thinking is indeed a rare commodity. The most important and challenging work involves thinking up the possibilities from which choices have to be made. The focus of effective strategic thinking is to gain a competitive product/market advantage, as discussed in Chapter 7 on the Value Matrix.

In *A Passion For Excellence*, Tom Peters recounts a story of John McConnell, chairman of Worthington Industries. Corporate procedure books at Worthington are replaced by a Golden Rule: "Take care of your customer and take care of your people, and the market will take care of you." Peters goes on to cite numerous examples of companies where employees don't need policy manuals or rule books to act ethically and fairly—they just do it. There are always a few who own values are flawed or expedient, but whom are nonetheless successful in the short term. In time, however, character flaws or even shortcomings like inconsistency do catch up with people, and as Peters says, those people are cast off like dandruff by their peers before they can cause serious problems for both the manager and the company. There is a basic assumption in such companies that part of their vision is a belief in human nature to work toward a vision when people understand the vision and live the message.

COMMUNICATION

Leaders with a true vision and a committed mission communicate about them at every opportunity. They use pictures, metaphors, parables, analogies, coaching, modeling, and any other device available at the moment. One curiosity here is that during the many years of consulting and teaching in this area, there are only a handful of people, and it seems as though they are the ones with truly visionary capabilities, who can transfer ideas from one industry to another. These people articulate ideas in a variety of ways, but are constantly cautious of being too ethereal or vague or constraining. Such constraint or abstraction causes confusion, frustration, demotivation, and cynicism.[10] Today, few employees know or care why their companies exist. Actions are committed only when embedded in broader organizational purpose, and most CEOs are well aware of this. Employees must identify with a purposeful organization, with people who care and who focus on intent.

An example can be found in Komatsu, the giant Japanese heavy equipment manufacturer. Their first articulated vision during the 1980s was to "surround Caterpillar." This was really more of a strategy than a vision. When the company had obtained a substantial market share at the expense of Caterpillar, the worldwide industry leader, there was a need for a new thrust to avoid losing the rudder. Komatsu then adopted the 3Gs—"Growth, Global, Groupwide." Komatsu believed this allowed each manager the freedom to interpret the vision creatively. The communication method is reminiscent of the long-standing AIDA model in marketing employed by Komatsu—Get people's *A*ttention, develop their *I*nterest, that is followed by *D*esire, and finally the *A*ction to make it happen. Instilling organizational values requires that people identify with them before extraordinary effort ensues. In less esoteric terms, you must sow before you can harvest. It provides a reason for people to commit, and few people would rather work for a company than belong to an organization. It requires a commitment to developing customers, employees, and relationships with diverse stakeholders.

PUTTING IT ALL TOGETHER

An explanation of an idea is often blurred by the academic context necessary to delineate the elements of the idea. As an example of an attempt in the banking industry to articulate the vision, mission, and culture of an organization we turn to Chase Manhattan Corp. Chase has a history that is on the one hand grandiose in the banking community, and on the other hand is fairly typical of the cultural stereotype that pervades the community. Following a dismal decade during the 1980s, it was painfully evident that a new direction was in order. The executive group, with a great deal of writhing and gnashing of teeth, agreed on a mission that Chase was to become the best financial-services provider in the world. Five values were outlined to support the mission: customer focus, respect for each other, teamwork, quality, and professionalism.

The saga continues, but before doing so, let's ask some difficult questions concerning the above situation. What is the vision? We have seen the delineation of a vision and mission become academic, so application of questions previously stated should help us sort out the difference. If Chase becomes the "best" provider of financial services by some rating device, will it be rudderless? Will their still be a *raison d'être*? The statement *does* put into words the desired future, it is brief; and it sets sights high. It *could* provide something worth risking for, instill commitment, be an anchor for consistency, permit alignment, and have accountability. It appears that the vision is reasonably well specified. Is the mission also covered in the statement? Financial services is what Chase will provide to its customers. So both vision and mission are within the single statement. Now we would ask what was different in terms of the "why" and "what" Chase was before articulation of the statement. Is there any change that would potentially reverse the dismal results of the recent past?

In terms of culture, the five values are a clear delineation of what Chase believes is important. They are communicating to all employees through meeting sessions. There are banners and coffee mugs and all the things that are necessary to keep the mission and values front and center. In terms of alignment, performance evaluations include a measure of adherence to the new statements, and cooperation among the bank's various business centers. Thomas G. Labrecque, president of Chase has been called a missionary for carrying the message to employees and customers. So everything seems to be in place at Chase, and still there is no guarantee of success, only a guarantee that if you don't take the risk you will fail. With the infrastructure in place, it is possible to move to some of the major alignment issues we will address in the chapters ahead as well as confrontation of the issues involved in change.

SOME CLOSING COMMENTS

Vision will assume greater significance in the decade ahead because it will be the source of sustained differential value advantage. The advantage is sourced in the vision and achieved through superior systems and through maximizing front-line decision competence and flexibility. Strategic vision encompasses a clear notion of which present and future value opportunities the bank will compete for and identifies specific concepts of how the bank will establish sustainable competitive positions based on these value opportunities. A vision of greatness allows people to enjoy what they do and get really excited about it. This is especially important for banking and professional services where "friendly banker" has become an oxymoron. There is a desperate need to stimulate curiosity and learning that leads to continual improvement akin to Schumpeter's concept of creative destruction. The world is full of persnickety customers and corporate momentum maulers, but life should be more than a continuous battle against pain. It needs to be a constant critical reexamination. The bottom line for vision is if management can't define it, employees, customers, or suppliers can't be expected to deliver it.

Endnotes

1. Schumpeter, Joseph A. (1942) *Capitalism, Socialism and Democracy*. NY: Harper & Bros.

2. Langeler, Gerald H. (1992) "The Vision Trap," *Harvard Business Review*, (March–April), Cat: "Then it doesn't matter which way you go." pp. 46–55.

3. Bibb, Porter. (1993) *"It Ain't As Easy As It Looks: Ted Turner's Story,"* NY: Crown Publishers.

4. Pearson, Andrall E. (1989) "Six Basics For General Managers," *Harvard Business Review*, (July–August), pp. 94–101.

5. *Business Week*. (1994) "Bill Gates Vision," (June 27), pp. 57–62.

6. Rayport, Jeffrey R. and John J. Sviolka. (1994) "Managing in the Marketspace," *Harvard Business Review*, (November–December), pp. 141–150.

7. Senge, Peter M. (1990) *The Fifth Discipline*, NY: Doubleday.

8. Levitt, Theodore. (1960) "Marketing Myopia," *Harvard Business Review*, (July–August).

9. *Forbes*. (1994) "What's His Secret?" (August 1), pp. 56–60.

10. Bartlett, Christopher A. and Sumantra Ghoshal. (1994) "Beyond Strategy To Purpose," *Harvard Business Review*, (November-December), pp. 79–88.

5. IDENTIFICATION OF VALUE OPPORTUNITIES

> "Competition for a sustainable differential value advantage is not about the formulation of plans for the future. It is about the identification of value opportunities and the effective implementation of plans."

T he industrial era has passed. We have moved through the service era and into the early stages of an emerging value era. Customers have greater access to information on product/service benefits enabling them to readily evaluate the value associated with competitive offerings.

What does all this change and transition mean for the commercial banking industry? It means that we must rethink the way we operate and manage in the new economy: It's not just business as usual. The ability to recognize this new economy, understand the roles of service, quality, and value in this new age, and anticipate the effects of these major changes are critical for success today and into the next century.

The commercial banking industry must make the transition from its more traditional service-based business to a value-driven business to effectively compete in the new era. This transaction requires a constant monitoring of the winds of change and understanding the consequences of change in order to be effectively positioned to capitalize on key opportunities. In a word: It means that you must be *proactive* not *reactive*.

The winds of change are ultimately driven by the marketplace—the behavior of customers and their needs. Environmental factors such as the behavior of competitors, technological advances, shifts in sociocultural mores and legal/political issues influence societal trends. The rate that these factors influence society and the way we do business, however, ultimately depends on the customer and what the customer values. In order to understand the consequences of change it is necessary to understand the marketplace.

DELIVERING VALUE

Success in value differentiation is not industry dependent. Markets can be segmented and value differentiation achieved within any industry. For example, we would not expect the automobile and bottled water industries to have much in common, but value differentiation has proven successful in both. Mazda Motor Corporation and Evian Waters of France Inc. have both been able to successfully achieve market segmentation and value differentiation by adopting a value-driven philosophy of business.

As the fourth and last place Japanese automaker in the United States, Mazda adopted a marketing strategy that found a hole—a *value void*—in the domestic automotive market. Mazda embarked on a new strategy to be a premium marketer instead of a price marketer by developing products for specific markets with its introduction of the Mazda Miata in July of 1989. Priced at just $13,800, the Miata often sold well above the sticker price. Since the Miata, Mazda has revamped its entire car line and established a new luxury division with specific markets in mind.

Can we achieve value differentiation, growth, and profitability with a product that has no distinct or unique performance characteristics? For all intents and purposes Evian Water is no different from tap water other than the $1.50 per bottle the consumer pays for Evian. The story of Evian Water clearly demonstrates how market segmentation can be used to achieve value differentiation with a product lacking any actual performance differences.

Evian Water has achieved growth and profitability in the competitive and explosive bottled water market, an industry that is currently flooded with 400 to 500 brands by pursuing a niche marketing strategy. The company's strategy places an overall emphasis on health, but highlights the specific needs of, and product benefits sought by each market niche. Evian's overall umbrella market is everyone who drinks water, but specifically adults 18–49. This broad market is divided into subsegments based on the specific market's characteristics, needs, and behaviors. By identifying with the unique characteristics, needs, and behaviors of these targeted segments, Evian achieves value differentiation.

The success of Evian Water directly correlates with its adoption of an aggressive market orientation. The company recognized the opportunity to position an upscale, expensive product in health-conscious market segments. Understanding the unique needs of each market made it possible for Evian to establish clear objectives for each segment.

This book leads you through a creative and logical process for identifying value opportunities. The end goal is to implement programs that support your organization's overall goals and provide sustainable differential value for targeted customers.

WHY PLAN?

The reason for planning is to ensure the long-term, sustained viability of your organization. It requires focusing on the customer. In other words, you need to find ways to meet your customers' needs that will be difficult for competing financial service providers to match.

A *value void* is created when disparity exists between the product/service offering(s) of the organization and the product/service offering(s) desired or needed by the customer. A classic example of the effect of a value-void is the rapid decline of Kmart in recent years. Kmart was positioned as the number one retailer in the world with ten times the customer base of the nearest competitor. After rising to prominence, Kmart elected to focus on operations and ignore general market trends and changes. The organization maximized short-term profits but failed to consider the customer's value equation.

Kmart's strategy was successful in the short run but proved disastrous in the face of competition. One competitor in particular, Wal-mart, was able to align its value equation closer to the customer's value equation and within 10 years displaced Kmart as the world's largest retailer. Subsequently, Kmart was bumped to a distant number two spot on the discount retailing chart with the new leader, Wal-mart, far out in front.

Regardless of industry, product, or service, competitive organizations all have one thing in common: a desire or mission to succeed and achieve certain chosen goals. These goals may run the gamut from financial to human resources but all ultimately relate to maximizing the value of the organization. Successful companies exhibit one common trait: They are all market-driven companies. These companies identify appropriate market segments based upon specified criteria and develop plans to deliver value to these markets. Some companies adopt a market-driven philosophy in response to sluggish performance or failure to meet established goals and objectives while others are insightful and proactive (see Chapter 1).

Recognizing that a value void may exist is the first stage in identifying a value opportunity. The organization's and customers' value equations are not static. Without this understanding an organization will experience a widening gap in the value offered and value sought. The expansion of the value void leaves the organization vulnerable to competitive entry. The possible shifts in value equations leading to the creation of a value void are illustrated in Figure 5-1.

Figure 5-1
VALUE VOID CREATION

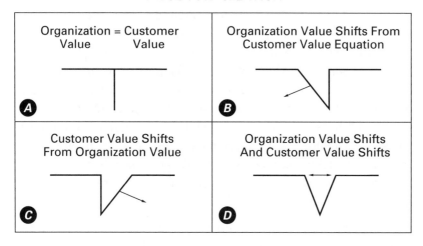

Initially, a successful organization's value offering is in line with the value sought by their targeted customers (A in Figure 5-1). This balance is indicative of those organizations that understand the relationship between strategic health and financial health. Over time the organization may shift focus, moving away from the customer's value equation and creating a void (B in Figure 5-1). This typically occurs when the organization begins to focus internally on operations. This shift to an internal focus, for example, cost control or cash flow, frequently results in a loss of vision and market perspective. Such an internal focus is indicative of those organizations that relegate strategic health to financial health. Once the equation is out of balance, the organization's internal focus exacerbates the value void between the value customers seek and the product/service being offered. From the customer's perspective the organization is continually decreasing the "value" delivered. This strategy may prove survivable in the short run, but the organization is vulnerable to competitive offerings more in line with the customer's value needs.

Imbalance in the value exchange might arise from a shift in the customer's value equation (C in Figure 5-1). Customers may be seeking more features or different benefits. If the organization is unwilling or unaware of the customer's value shift, a disparity between value provided and value sought emerges. Frequently, the organization's initial response to this possibility is denial: "No way this could ever happen." or "I know my customers." *Consumers cannot tell you about shifts in value preferences if you are not asking the right questions* (see Chapter 6). Due to internal or external influences, the organization may be unable, reluctant or unwilling to align with its customers' value shifts. The value void, however, will still exist. Organizational rationale and justification are irrelevant. Typical responses of commercial banks have been to "bridge this value void" with greater selling efforts. Short-term returns may result but this approach denies the fundamental problem.

A value void also occurs when the organization and customer both experience value shifts, but these value shifts are out of sync or in opposite directions (D in Figure 5-1). *Regardless of the reason for the emergence of a value void the result is competitive vulnerability.*

Planning, constantly monitoring your environment, and being aware of and understanding customer needs are the best and most effective ways to detect opportunities based on a value void. The organization able to recognize and anticipate shifts in customers' value equations will be postured to leverage a sustainable differential value advantage.

IDENTIFICATION OF VALUE OPPORTUNITIES

Wherever planning takes place, it is guided by the corporate vision and mission of the planning organization as described in Chapter 3. It involves a match between organization resources and differential value opportunities.

The process for identifying value opportunities is a series of simple, interconnected steps that build from one to the other.[1] By going through each step in this market-oriented approach to planning, your organization will be on the way to developing a strategy that is reflective of market needs and based on sustaining a real differential value advantage within the marketplace.

Step 1: Establish guiding vision statement and overall goals. Inventory and assess current resources and capabilities. The value infrastructure is the driving principle of what your bank wants to become in the long term and how it will serve its markets and stakeholders (see Chapters 3 and 4).

Step 2: Develop a matrix for Corporate and each Strategic Business Unit, showing product lines and corresponding markets served.

Step 3: Establish screening criteria for prioritization of products/markets (see Chapter 6, financial and strategic health measures). For each product/market that you determine as a priority, follow steps 4 and 5.

Step 4: Complete analysis of customer needs and behaviors; prepare an analysis of strengths and weakness of competitors.

Step 5: Identify and select key opportunities for sustainable differential value advantage.

Guiding Principles and Purpose

Anybank, USA is a small rural commercial bank with a population base of approximately 20,000 and moderate resources. Anybank, USA adopted the following vision statement and guiding principles:

Vision Statement

Make Anybank, USA the bank of first choice for customers seeking "small-town hospitality" and value.

Guiding Principles

1. Assure superior customer service for all customers at a fair and reasonable price.

2. Maintain a safe and rewarding environment for all our employees.

3. Create a positive economic impact on Anybank through sustainable growth.

Anybank's vision reflects some introspection on the part of the planning organization. They have considered their position in relation to competitors and what Anybank can offer customers. Also, they have briefly stated their intended purpose. They could have been a little more thorough on their guiding principles, however. For instance, what about the community at large? Remember, guiding principles are standards that cannot be violated and help keep your plan on track with your overall purpose.

Product/Market Matrix

Every commercial bank serves a set of markets by offering products and services. Today's turbulent marketplace will require commercial banks to provide differential value for their markets or lose out to those who will provide that value. A Product/Market Matrix is a useful tool for setting priorities and allowing you to focus on those areas where the greatest returns are expected as a result of a sustainable value advantage.

In order to understand the Product/Market (P/M) Matrix, a couple of definitions are helpful. First, a product is defined from a customer's point of view and can be a "product line" or singular offering. The goods, services, or events within a product line should be seen as satisfying essentially the same set of customer needs and should be relatively "interchangeable" from the customer's perspective.

For example, a product line in the travel industry called "Resort Facilities" might make sense because customers see every resort facility in the line as meeting the same specific set of needs. A product line, simply called lodging—inclusive of motels, hotels, convention, and resort facilities—makes less sense because the needs satisfied by a motel differ from the needs satisfied by a major resort or conference facility. The customer does not see motel and resort as interchangeable in the value offered and received.

Always keep in mind the way a customer sees a product or service, otherwise your marketing efforts will confuse the customer.

Anybank, USA identified the following product lines:

Deposit Accounts	Secured Credit	Unsecured Credit
Auto Loans	College Loans	Credit Cards
Mortgages	Trusts	

Second, a market is defined as a group of customers with needs that respond to a specific product or service offering. Needs and behaviors of customers within a market should be similar. Needs and behaviors of customers in separate markets should show some differences. No two markets should have customers with identical needs. If you find two markets with the same needs and behaviors, the two markets should be combined into one market for planning purposes.

At a basic level markets can be divided on a purely geographic basis. It is unlikely that customer needs are equivalent across all demographic variables within any regional/geographic market definition. It is best, however, in initial efforts to determine total markets rather than market segments in the P/M Matrix. As you get better market information you will be able to refine your identification of markets and market segments. The P/M Matrix provides focus for identifying potential opportunities. When evaluating your markets, it is useful to apply the following criteria for market definition:

- a common set of needs within the market;
- distinct differences in needs among markets;
- reachable (via common communication/promotion lines/distribution channels); and
- substantial (large enough to be profitable).

85

Anybank, USA identified five retail markets with the following characteristics:

- *Young Singles:* white collar lower income, above average education with no kids.
- *Influential Families:* married with kids, white collar and professional workers, upper income and high education.
- *Mid-America Couples:* married without kids at home, average education, lower income, somewhat older.
- *Influential Couples:* married without kids at home, white collar and professional workers, upper income and high education.
- *Separated Singles:* divorced/widowed without kids at home, average education, above average income, slightly older.

These market definitions are better than geographic definitions because they reflect distinct markets with separate needs, behaviors, characteristics, and above all value definitions. These markets represent potential customers for Anybank, USA from any geographic area. Anybank could break these markets down further into geographic clusters as they get better information. Targeting geographically is more of a tactical decision involving communication strategies and typical travel distances. For now, however, it is best for Anybank to adhere to the above five markets.

Anybank, USA identified two commercial markets defined as large (50 or more employees) and small (less than 50 employees). Anybank's markets consist of the following identifiable groups:

SBU:	RETAIL DIVISION	COMMERCIAL DIVISION
Markets	• Young Singles	• Large Commercial
	• Influential Families	• Small Commercial
	• Mid-America Couples	
	• Influential Couples	
	• Separated Singles	

The use of these identifiable markets works well for the small bank in this example. In a larger corporation this analysis would be better if developed at a business unit level.

Now that Anybank has identified their product offerings and markets they can put the two together. Listing the products down the left side and markets across the top forms a matrix (Figure 5-2). Each intersecting cell in the matrix constitutes a Product/ Market. For example, the Product/Market (P/M) labeled A in Figure 5-2 represents the influential families market for college loans. The product /market labeled B in Figure 5-2 represents the influential couples market for auto loans.

Figure 5-2
CORPORATE PRODUCT/MARKET MATRIX
Anybank, USA

SBU:	RETAIL DIVISION					COMMERCIAL DIVISION	
Markets / **Products**	Young Singles	Influential Families	Mid-America Couples	Influential Couples	Separated Singles	Large Commercial	Small Commercial
Deposit Accounts							
Secured Credit							
Unsecured Credit							
Auto Loans				B			
College Loans		A					
Credit Cards							
Mortgages							
Trusts							

Once we have developed our overall "Corporate Product/Market Matrix," an environmental scan is conducted to identify trends that could have an impact on some or all Product/Markets. A systematic identification of trends is essential to be proactive rather than reactive. Types of factors that might impact the Product/Markets include:

- Political and Legal
- Economic
- Social and Cultural
- Competitive
- Organization Resources
- Secondary Service Providers

The key to understanding the environment is to keep an open mind and look for general trends, patterns, and/or key events that may affect the markets you serve and/or the products you offer. Beyond recognition of these trends, the organization must anticipate the outcome of changes in the environment. Predicting the graying of America does not require a futurist. The question remains—"How will the graying of America affect the value offerings of commercial banks?" What are the consequences of this change on the identification, creation, and delivery of customer value?

Strategic Business Units

Most commercial banks are too diverse to have one, overall plan. Successful planning in a competitive environment requires focusing on products and markets. In order to simplify the planning process and maintain a market orientation, you may want to subdivide your resources into smaller planning units called "Strategic Business Units" (SBUs). Once you have developed a corporate Product/Market Matrix you will have a better understanding of your SBUs.

Every SBU serves a number of markets with specific product lines. Each product line should be defined from the customer's point of view as a family of products that satisfies essentially the same set of needs. Planning at the Strategic Business Unit level answers the question "How should we compete?"

There is no formula for dividing organizational resources into planning units. This is an organizational decision with the objective of improving planning in order to compete on the basis of value in the marketplace. Ideally, an SBU exhibits the following characteristics:

1. It has its own mission, subordinate to the corporate mission.

2. It is made up of related products and markets.

3. It has its own competitors.

4. It is planned for independent of other business initiatives.

5. It is a profit center.

In Figure 5-2, the product/market matrix contains two basic SBUs: a Retail SBU and a Commercial SBU.

Prioritizing Product/Markets

Once a clear perspective on products and markets has been developed, the next step is to overlay the organization's vision as the first criteria in evaluating the Product/Market Matrix.

The purpose of the Product/Market Matrix provides a framework for identifying differential value opportunities and to prioritize them. Each P/M cell represents a value opportunity of varying quality. We must prioritize so we can focus our planning efforts on the Product/Markets most important to meeting our goals. Screening criteria are simply standards or parameters that the organization uses to evaluate each P/M. It's up to you to decide what "screening criteria" to put into each cell in order to prioritize Product/Markets for planning. Some examples of screening criteria might include:

Strategic Health Criteria

- customer counts
- market growth
- competitive value index

Financial Health Criteria

- fee income generation
- deposit dollars
- service charges
- commission income generation

Be sure the numbers you use are not simply "guesses." If you do not know the "answer," leave it blank, recognizing that this is an area where you have an information shortfall. Selection of screening criteria should not be limited to readily accessible information. At this point it is important to recognize that you may not know everything and realize that you will get better information as you mature through the planning process. Do not get stuck searching for "all the answers" and failing to plan because you are spending all your time collecting data. Make the best decisions with the information you have and include better data collection as part of your plan.

The selection of screening criteria is extremely important and should be made with great care. These criteria will set the priorities for your SBU and drive your P/M objectives. As a result, your selection of screening criteria should be made without consideration of what information can presently be provided. Once you have decided on the appropriate screening criteria, you can work to acquire the necessary information. Your information should be made to serve you, not the other way around.

Our fictitious organization, Anybank, USA, chose five screening criteria to prioritize Product/Markets for the Retail Division (SBU):

1. customer counts
2. competitive value index
3. market growth
4. income generation
5. service charges

To prioritize the potential of the Product/Markets for the retail division, Anybank, USA collected information on customer counts, competitive value, market growth, income generation, and service charges. For customer counts, fee income, and service charges, Anybank, USA was able to get the information from operating statements and other internal sources. The competitive value index and market growth required additional research and the use of external sources of information.

Recognizing the need for additional information, Anybank, USA evaluated market growth on a scale using low, moderate, and high. The competitive value index was initially generated on a scale from 1 to 5, with 5 representing high competitive value (from the customer's perspective). The measures of market growth and competitive value, though lacking the precision of fee income, service charges, or customer counts are extremely beneficial for the bank since they recognize the need for better information while incorporating what they presently know. In Figure 5-3, the Product/Market for Mid-America Couples/Auto Loans has been highlighted to show the application of Anybank, USA's screening criteria.

As we said before, Anybank, USA is a small rural commercial bank with a population base of approximately 20,000 and moderate resources. These screening criteria, however, can be used with any level of planning: local, regional, state, national, or multi-national organizations. The selection of the appropriate screening criteria is not necessarily dependent upon the level at which you are planning, but on the overall goals you have set and the particular SBU you are developing. Think about the broad-ranged goals you have set and the way you have defined your SBUs. Then determine the criteria that will best help you identify opportunities to meet your goals. Again, do not become bogged down searching for "all data," but do identify ways to capture information for the future. A note of caution: Be careful of seasonal variances in applying criteria to Product/Markets. Seasonal variation may not be reflected in partial year numbers.

Figure 5-3
PRODUCT/MARKET MATRIX
Retail Division: Anybank, USA

Markets / Products	Young Singles	Influential Families	Mid-America Couples	Influential Couples	Separated Singles	TOTALS
Deposit Accounts						
Secured Credit						
Unsecured Credit						

Auto Loans			#cust = 100
			CVI = 3
			MG = Low
			Inc = $114K
			Svc$<1K			

College Loans						
Credit Cards						
Mortgages						
Trusts						
TOTALS						

Product/Market Criteria: #cust - customer count; CVI - competitive value index (5 high value);
MG - market growth (low, moderate, high); Inc - income generation; Svc$ - services charges.

When completed, the Product/Market Matrix allows you to see which markets deserve more attention. Is fee generation in one Product/Market lagging behind other Product/Markets? Is there an opportunity to boost deposits by focusing on two key Product/Markets? It is critical that careful attention be given to the selection and application of screening criteria before comparisons can be made between Product/Markets for a Strategic Business Unit (see Chapter 6).

Key Questions

The following is a checklist to make sure you have correctly developed your Product/Market Matrix:

- Is every product line defined from the customer's point of view?

- Do customers within a market have a common set of needs?

- Are there similarities in needs within the markets and differences in needs between markets?

- Have you selected important, relevant data to include in the Product/Market Matrix as screening criteria?

- Are you using current, real information and not potential or "guesses?"

- Have you used this information to select priority Product/Markets on which to concentrate your time and resources?

Understanding Customer Needs and Competition

Understanding customer behavior is important for a number of reasons. First, it helps ensure that each of your products and services fills a market need. You can tailor your accessibility, pricing, and communication programs to the way your customers want to do business. Second, it helps you determine whether you have correctly identified markets on your Product/Market Matrix. Third, it makes it easier to identify meaningful strengths and weaknesses and those of your competition.

What Do Customers Value?

Customers have "qualifying needs" and "determining needs." Qualifying needs must be satisfied before the customer will even consider visiting your bank. After using qualifying needs to select a list of possible commercial banks, the customer uses determining needs, things he or she would like to have, to make the final decision.

An example of house-hunting illustrates the difference between qualifying and determining needs (Figure 5-4). A married couple in their early 30s with two pre-teenage children is interested in

93

buying a house. They explain to their realtor that there are certain things the house they buy must have. The house must cost no more than $95,000, have more than one bathroom, have at least three bedrooms, and be in a good school district. No house is acceptable to this couple unless it meets these criteria. These are *qualifying needs*. The realtor can use qualifying needs to choose a selection of houses for the couple to consider.

Figure 5-4
QUALIFYING AND DETERMINING NEEDS
Home Purchase Example

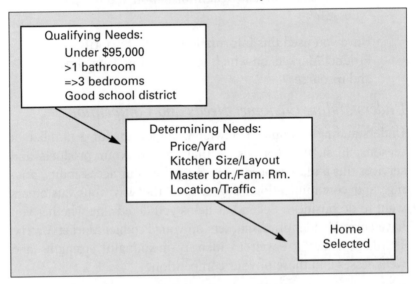

The couple now considers things they would like to have. They might like a large eat-in kitchen, master bedroom, family room, fireplace, large yard, not too much traffic on the street, and a two-car garage. These are *determining needs*. No house may meet all of these determining needs perfectly. One house might have the best kitchen, while another has the fireplace and yard they want. The couple must trade off one feature for another and find the best compromise to suit their needs. This is the house they will buy. In essence, the couple has determined the house offering the greatest value after meeting initial qualifying criteria.

Some attributes might be included as both qualifying needs and determining needs. Price often works this way. For example, a customer may tell the travel agent he will not pay a 20 percent premium for a deluxe suite. This is a qualifying need. Within that 20 percent margin, however, price becomes a determining need— the lower the price, the more attractive the purchase becomes.

Ask the Customer

In putting together a market needs analysis, list qualifying and determining needs specific to the product/market for which you are planning. Find out what these needs are by talking to customers. Do not rely on your intuition. List these needs in descending order of importance to the customer.

Be careful that your market needs analysis lists true customer needs, not just a list of product/service features. Think in terms of benefits the customer will receive from your organization. For example, the customer does not have a "need" for a 24-hour automatic teller machine; the customer needs convenience and availability of funds. One way of satisfying that need is a 24-hour automatic teller machine.

The N of 1 Approach?

All too frequently we hear statements like—"The other day Joe told me..." or "At church Sue said..."—as evidence for decision-making and justification. The inherent risk of relying solely on anecdotal evidence of customer needs is a corporate action that shifts the bank away from its customer base and creates a void between the customer's value equation and the organization. One should never ignore input from customers, but caution should be exercised in any translation of single case views to corporate action. One can and should use much of this information to help structure focus groups to get a better understanding of customer needs.

Focus groups provide an unstructured forum for current customers, potential customers, and/or lost customers to communicate their needs and views. Focus groups are widely used to collect information in an unstructured and indirect interview format. Groups of eight to 10 customers are brought together to discuss issues in an unstructured format. This technique is used primarily for the definition of problems and to provide background information rather than to provide solutions for problems. Focus groups are ideally suited for the generation of ideas for improving products or services, and information collected from focus groups can be used to help structure questions for a larger scale and more definitive, generalizable collection of information.

The better you identify customer needs (the components of their value equation), the more creative you will be in finding solutions to those needs that set you apart from the competition.

Key Questions

Ask yourself the following questions to make sure you have accurately and completely identified product/market needs.

Product/Market Needs

- Do you view the world through the customer's eyes?
- Are customer needs you have identified specific to the Product/Market?
- Are customer needs described as precisely as possible? Have you avoided listing general needs that could apply to any Product/Market?
- Have you divided customer needs into qualifying and determining needs? Is this accurate from the customer's point of view?
- Have you distinguished between true customer needs and product features?
- Are determining needs listed in descending order of importance to the customer?
- What benefits do customers seek?
- What factors influence customer behaviors?
- What is the customers' basis for comparisons with other offerings?

- What risks does the customer perceive?
- How do customers bank?
- How does banking fit into their lifestyles?
- How often do customers require banking services?
- Where do customers seek information?
- Why do customers bank where they do?

Competitive Analysis

Detailed competitive analysis shows your competitive value position within a specific Product/Market by examining customer counts, market share, and the marketing mix elements for each of the leading competitors in the market. The marketing mix elements are the four key tools—product/service, price, distribution/location, and promotion—that interact to form a comprehensive value offering to the marketplace.

To begin, tabulate assets for your competitors as well as for your own organization specific to the particular Product/Market that is targeted for planning. Use figures specific to the targeted Product/Market. Much of this data is available from state, federal, private sources, or simple observation of competitive offerings.

Next, list the percentage of market for yourself and each competitor for this specific Product/Market. This gives you a quick comparison of how one competitor is faring against the others. Indicate whether each competitor's market share is increasing, decreasing, or staying the same. By analyzing market trends, along with marketing mix elements, you are able to determine why each organization's strategy has been more or less effective in this Product/Market. Now consider the marketing mix for each organization. Remember the four elements that make up the marketing mix. Comment only on those elements where a competitive advantage or disadvantage exists for yourself and your competitors:

1. Product line features and benefits.

2. Price policies and strategies.

3. Location and service delivery.

4. Promotion policies and activities.

Again, you should list only "differentiation factors" that distinguish one organization's marketing mix from the other's. Remember, these should be done from the customer's point of view. Also, list only critically distinguishing factors—do not list common features. For example, if all commercial banks in the area offer "free checking" that is not a differentiating factor among them and will not be listed under product line.

If there are few differentiating factors identified after completing the competitive analysis either (1) the competitors in that Product/Market are not doing much to differentiate themselves or (2) competitors are doing something that you do not know about. For example, if a competing bank has experienced substantial growth in assets and you have not identified any special differentiating marketing mix characteristics, you need to do more research.

Key Questions

Answer the following questions for each P/M to make sure you have considered all salient issues concerning the competition:

Who are the key competitors in this Product/Market?

For each competitor, consider the following questions:

- Are their prices/rate structures above or below ours?
- How do their price policies and strategies compare?
- What customer needs do they fill that we do not?
- What geographic markets do they attract?
- How do they communicate with their customers?
- Do customers see this competitor's products/services as superior or inferior to ours?
- Have you identified factors that differentiate your competitors from each other, as opposed to factors they have in common?

- Did you list differentiation factors from the customer's point of view?
- Do you have hard data about your competitors, or are you relying too much on your intuition?
- Are your market weaknesses inferred from your competitors' strengths?
- Are your market strengths listed the same as your differentiation factors?
- Do customers agree with your analysis of your market strengths and weaknesses?

Value Opportunities

The analysis to this point reveals your organization's capabilities, talents, and skills in this Product/Market, and how you can use these unique capabilities, talents, and skills to create or enhance a sustainable value advantage.

Use your marketing mix differentiation factors (product/service, distribution, promotion, price) from the competitive analysis to identify your strengths in descending order of importance for the market. Your strengths are those areas that you identified as differentiating your organization from your competitors. These strengths will help you identify value opportunities.

While it's best to lead from strength, it's also important to list your critical weaknesses in descending order of importance. This is particularly important if a weakness relates to meeting a qualifying need. If that's the case, this too presents a value opportunity and you must correct that weakness before you can effectively compete in this market.

You can infer your market weaknesses by looking at the differentiation factors for your competitors. A competing organization's strength implies that you have a relative weakness on that particular point.

A *value opportunity* is any match between an organizational strength (value advantage) and a market need (customers' value components). A strategy that leads by improving a weakness (value disadvantage) often is more expensive and appears as a "me-too" approach. Customers need a reason to bank with you, and "me too" is not a good reason. What you are really looking for is a "differential value advantage" over competing financial service providers. Figure 5-5 provides a useful way to think about value opportunities.

Figure 5-5
VALUE OPPORTUNITY GRID

	CUSTOMER'S QUALIFYING NEEDS: SCREENING VALUE EQUATION	CUSTOMER'S DETERMINING NEEDS: DECISION VALUE EQUATION
BANK STRENGTH: VALUE ADVANTAGE	Makes no sense to improve here.	Leverage for differential value advantage.
BANK WEAKNESS: VALUE DISADVANTAGE	Critical to qualify for consideration.	May be necessary to improve if related need is very important

The real key to winning is to find new and creative ways to leverage your value advantages within the customer's value decision framework for affecting a sustainable differential value advantage (Figure 5-5, upper right-hand corner of the diagram). This can happen once you qualify for consideration (Figure 5-5, upper left-hand corner). By fulfilling the basic requirements of the customer's screening value equation the bank qualifies as part of the customer's set of alternatives. If the bank does not qualify for consideration it is advantageous to correct value disadvantages that are used as part of the customer's qualifying screening equation (Figure 5-5, lower left-hand corner).

Competition for customers is intensive and concentrated among competitors who have qualified for consideration. Once qualified, the bank competes by leveraging value advantages (Figure 5-5, upper right-hand corner). Sometimes you must correct a *value disadvantage* related to a very important determining need (decision value equation) before the customer will consider your *value advantages* (Figure 5-5, lower right-hand corner). Remember, however, that correcting a value disadvantage is unlikely to be the main focus of your efforts. Winners lead from strength.

Once you have identified all of the value opportunities, rank them in descending order of importance. Remember, opportunities address market needs identified in the P/M cell under investigation. Identifying and understanding the relative importance of customers' needs in relationship to your value advantages enables you to focus resources where they will have maximum positive effect. Customers will value and be willing to pay for what you are doing (process outcomes) when you align the organization's value equation with the customer's value equation.

Key Questions

Value Opportunities

- Does every value opportunity you have identified address a real need customers have?

- Have you looked to your strengths first in identifying value opportunities, rather than promoting efforts to improve on weaknesses?

- If a market weakness prevents you from effectively competing in the market, are you doing anything to fix the situation?

- Does the value opportunity identified have face validity? Did you move logically from one step to the next?

- Does it fit with the vision, guiding principles, and goals of your organization and the specific SBU?

- Is it feasible? Can you implement it?

- Is the value opportunity understandable? Is every opportunity clear, not subject to more than one interpretation?

• Can you trace every value opportunity back to a specific market need?

• Is the value opportunity based on accurate market information, especially regarding market needs and the competing financial service providers?

SUMMARY

You have done a lot of work to identify differential value opportunities! Now there are a lot of people who need to know about it. First, communicate with everyone in your organization. Every key person should understand the identified opportunities, programs, timetable, and performance measurements.

Customers also need to know. Market strategies are what differentiate competitors in the marketplace. Your customers need to know how you are different. Leverage your differential value for a sustainable competitive advantage. Give customers a reason for using your services.

Organizations that have been successful in living the process of value differentiation follow these 10 rules:

1. Divide your organization into clearly defined Strategic Business Units (SBUs). The number of SBUs and what they include will vary from organization to organization.

2. Give great care and considerable thought to selecting data to prioritize Product/Markets. This will set priorities for the entire organization.

3. Create a Product/Market Matrix for every SBU. This will allow you to identify the priority Product/Markets.

4. Collect the information you need to effectively plan right now. Critically important areas are customer needs, customer behavior, and what competitors are doing in the market. You already may have much of the information you need. However, getting some of it may require formal market research.

5. Select teams. Each team should represent a variety of responsibilities within the organization. They should clearly understand the process of value opportunity identification. People who participate in identifying the value opportunities will feel more responsible for accomplishing the objectives. Dictating an action rarely results in success.

6. Identify a champion of the process. This is the person that keeps the process moving. He or she should have leadership ability, direct access to organization leaders, an understanding of the process, and outstanding communication skills. Select this person with care.

7. Establish a specific timetable for identifying, reviewing, and revising differential value opportunities identified through the process. Opportunities must be identified for every high-priority Product/Market in each SBU. This takes time and is rarely perfect the first time. Without a timetable, the process is ignored while team members deal with day-to-day crises.

8. The organization must establish a formal review process. This provides several benefits:

    - It demonstrates commitment to the process.
    - The quality of the opportunities identified improves when team members know others will see the result.
    - It ensures opportunities fit with the organization's vision.
    - It ensures that enough money, manpower, and other resources will be applied to leverage the value opportunity for sustainable differential advantage.
    - It is an alignment check to ensure your organization is aligned with the vision.

9. Communicate the process and outcomes with everyone in your organization.

10. Develop measures of financial and strategic health. Financial measures determine whether the opportunity is contributing to the organization. Strategic health measures determine how the market thinks you are performing relative to competition. It is possible to do well financially and be extremely vulnerable to competition. On the other hand, a new value differentiation strategy may require time to generate financial returns. The only way to be sure you are heading in the right direction is to monitor your strategic health on a continual basis. If your strategy provides sustainable value advantages, your organization will ultimately be both strategically and financially healthy.

Times have changed. Having a "good" product no longer guarantees success. Success will go to commercial banks that provide "differential value" for the customer. That requires accurate information, understanding the consequences of change, effectively planning, and successfully implementing your plan.

The commercial banking industry must make the transition from a service-based business to a value-based business to effectively compete in the new economy. This means we must constantly monitor the winds of change, understand the consequences of change, and be positioned to capitalize on key opportunities. In a word: It means that we must be *proactive*.

A value void is created when a disparity exists between the product/service offering(s) of the organization and the product/service offering(s) desired or needed by the customer. Recognizing that a value void may exist is the first stage in a change in philosophy. The organization's and customers' value equations are not static. Without this understanding an organization will experience a widening gap in the value offered and value sought. The emergence or expansion of the value void leaves the organization vulnerable to competitive entry. The aim of the organization should be to maintain propinquity between the organization's and customers' value equations.

Endnotes

1. For a comprehensive, indepth discussion of the strategic marketing planning process for banking see: *The Bank Marketing Handbook,* by R. Eric Reidenbach, Chicago: Probus, 1994.

6. Strategic Value Measurement

> "If we can't
> measure it,
> we can't
> manage it."
> -Anon

T he shift to a new paradigm, with the attendant shift in philosophical orientation, requires new thinking about the nature of relevant, important outcomes and the types of measures necessary to evaluate progress toward those outcomes. A production orientation, for example, would emphasize measures of efficiency and uniformity—and the result of such measures would be limited offerings provided as efficiently as possible. A sales orientation would typically emphasize measures such as revenue growth and market share, and might include process measures such as cross-selling effectiveness and motivational factors. A market orientation, as discussed in Chapter 1, would include measures of customer service effectiveness and, possibly, embryonic measures of customer satisfaction.

Underlying all of these business philosophies, however, is a strong—if separate—reliance on financial measures to assess the ultimate health of the bank. Short-term profits, ROE,

ROA, and efficiency ratios typically become the measures used to assess the effectiveness of a bank's strategy and its place in the banking community.[1] Although these financial measures are necessary and important, they are inadequate, in themselves, for evaluating the strategic health of a bank or of any company. This is particularly true at a time when management is embracing a new philosophy of business, articulating a new value infrastructure, and embarking on a new strategy targeted at high value-opportunity markets. If the organization changes and the measurement system doesn't, the result will be measures that are, at best, ineffective and, at worst, counterproductive. We believe that a value orientation requires a comprehensive, integrative set of "results" and "process" measures designed to assess both the financial health and the strategic health of the bank.

FINANCIAL AND STRATEGIC HEALTH

Traditional financial measures such as return on investment or equity or assets, sales growth, and operating income provide useful indicators of business performance—from the perspective of the rear-view mirror. *Financial measures typically are lagging indicators*; they can be useful in reflecting the effects of past strategies and practices but have limited diagnostic value and are virtually useless in attempts to predict the future results of bold, new strategies. In this respect, measures of the financial health of banks are analogous to measures of human temperature: Normal temperatures don't necessarily indicate that all is well, while abnormal temperatures, in the absence of other indicators, provide little in the way of diagnostic information. In fact, during periods of transition resulting from changes in the business environment or changes in a bank's strategic direction, financial measures, by themselves, are more likely to mislead than to enlighten.

Measures of strategic health are leading indicators of future financial health; they provide a view through the windshield rather than through the rear-view mirror. Measures of strategic health provide readings of all facets of the business environment—including the bank's competitive position—*from the customer's point of view.* The word "customer" is used here to provide focus. In point of fact, "customer" is properly defined as "all members of the targeted market," whether or not they currently do business with your bank. Measures of customer satisfaction *can* serve as primary indicators of strategic health, although it will be argued that the current practice of customer satisfaction measurement in banking is embryonic and, as such, can be as misleading as reliance on measures of financial health alone. Moreover, typical measures of customer satisfaction focus exclusively on the numerator of the value equation (benefits sought by the customer), failing to adequately take into account the actual or perceived price to the customer of those benefits. In addition, current banking practice is typically focused on a single bank, ignoring the strategic health of its competitors. This single bank focus leads to a very limited and incomplete view of the bank's *true* strategic health. *Market perceptions* of relative value, therefore, represent more powerful indicators of strategic health than even multifaceted measures of "customer satisfaction" as they are currently applied in most segments of services industries.[2] We will discuss the implications of these and other measures of strategic and financial health in this chapter and will provide further ramifications of value measurement in Chapter 7.

The importance of distinguishing between measures of strategic and financial health cannot be overstated. We do *not* take the position, put forth by many consultants, that you should simply forget financial measures, concentrating instead upon operational measures and taking on faith that financial results will follow. However, we do argue that financial measures must be only one component of a broader set of measures, the latter including measures of strategic health. Moreover, measures of strategic health must be given *greater* emphasis than financial measures in determining and evaluating strategy, designing compensation systems, and in procedures designed for employee performance appraisals. Until that happens, to quote the CEO of Analog Devices, "When conflicts arise, financial considerations win out."[3]

A privately held, local bank that was recently acquired by a neighboring bank at a fraction of its potential value, asked us to participate in a post-mortem marketing audit. Distilling the available information into indications of strategic and financial health over a 10-year period resulted in the following picture depicted in Figure 6-1.

Figure 6-1
FINANCIAL VERSUS STRATEGIC HEALTH OF MVB
(Myopic Vision Bank)

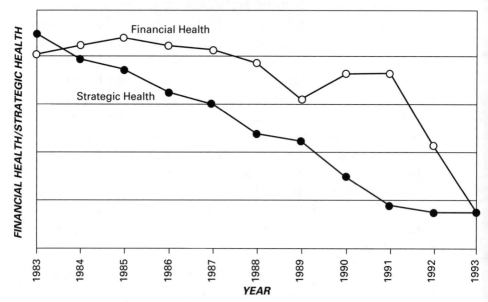

Although not systematically collected, this bank did have indicators of strategic health in the form of customer complaints, customer defections, and employee dissatisfaction. The financial indicators, that the bank used exclusively for performance reviews, included profitability, ROA, and efficiency ratios.

The post-mortem audit revealed that, although the bank's financial position continued to grow through 1985, the various indicators of strategic health were already declining two years earlier. During the late 1980s the bank attempted to improve its financial position through enhanced sales efforts, investing heavily in cross-selling techniques and employee motivation. By 1989, facing significant financial decline, the bank's officers decided that costs were out of control and they entered into a period of downsizing. Encouraged by the improved financial results, they continued to "explain away" rising customer complaints, rationalizing that this was simply part of "the new reality." Had the bank managers recognized the importance of strategic health, utilizing these and other more proactive measures to evaluate the causes of their declining financial health, they could have made appropriate course corrections and averted the fatal spiral that they experienced. In fact, the new owners have done a strategic health analysis, and have realigned their own core capabilities to enhance customer value in this market, with predictably positive results.

An example from another of our clients demonstrates appropriate use of strategic and financial health measures in combination. The client, a Fortune 500 company, recognized that *something* was wrong as early as 1985 when sales and profits began to decline from previous periods of growth. Acknowledging that financial indicators were merely a symptom of potentially substantive underlying problems, management began to systematically gather customer satisfaction information in 1986 in order to better understand the needs of their targeted market and their own competitive position from the market's viewpoint. Detailed analyses of this information led to the realization that existing strategy was out of alignment with the evolving needs of the market. Faced with the decision to "sell harder" or to embark on a bold new strategy designed to provide customer value, our client made the tough decision to provide increased customer benefits at reduced cost. The new value strategy was formulated in 1987 and implemented in 1988. (See Figure 6-2.)

The point of this example is that sales and profits did not *immediately* respond to the change of strategy, although customers perceived improved performance relative to their needs, and increased value relative to the competition. The challenge for management, in this case, was to focus attention and internal rewards on performance relative to strategic health, while monitoring but de-emphasizing financial performance in the short term. Had they failed to meet this challenge, the company may have abandoned the new strategy prematurely or, at the least, have curtailed investment in the new strategy. Attention to strategic health information, including a carefully designed set of customer value measures, proved the guiding force in determining both "what was wrong" and in determining where to invest for maximum improvement.

Figure 6-2
THE RELATIONSHIP BETWEEN GROSS PROFIT AND CUSTOMER SATISFACTION FOR CTHELITE CORP.

Another point to be drawn from this example is that financial health *does* follow from good strategic health. As described in Chapter 2, a differential value advantage (good strategic health) affects an organization's performance through:

- customer retention;
- reduced price elasticities;

- lower costs of customer acquisition;
- lower direct costs; and/or
- enhanced firm reputation.

The linkage between strategic and financial health can be demonstrated empirically in Figure 6-3.[4]

Figure 6-3
THE VALUE OF CUSTOMER SATISFACTION

DATA/FACTS

- Ten percent of bank customers leave per year.
- Twenty-one percent of that 10 percent leave due to poor service.
- Each bank customer = $121 gross profit/year.
- Cost to acquire new customer = $150.

RESULTS (for a bank that has 200,000 customers)

20,000 leave x .21 (poor service) = 4,200 customers

x $121 gross profit per customer = $508,200

+ cost of replacing lost customers (4,200 x $150) = $630,000

Annual Cost of Poor Service $1,138,200

Source: *American Banking Association, May 1990 report.*

If we were also to factor in the findings of the TARP studies referenced in Chapter 2, namely that each dissatisfied customer is likely to tell nine other people of his/her dissatisfaction, the true value of customer satisfaction would be several times higher than the figure reported by the American Banking Association.

The Case for Proactive Measures

The experience of our Myopic Vision Bank, discussed earlier, clearly illustrates the importance of emphasizing strategic health over financial indicators. Despite the reactive nature of the strategic health indicators used in the post-mortem analysis, MVB would have benefited significantly by noting that its strategy was clearly not providing the benefits valued by its customers—as evidenced by the number of complaints and customer defections. But would these reactive indicators have been sufficient for determining and implementing a new, value-driven strategy? Do customer complaints adequately reflect the range of benefits considered important by customers? Do *customer* complaints adequately reflect the concerns of *potential customers* currently doing business with a competitor?

As previously noted in Chapter 2, the TARP studies concluded that only 4 percent of dissatisfied customers actually complain to management. The bank that relies solely on customer complaints to assess strategic health, therefore, is essentially ignoring the possible dissatisfaction of up to 96 percent of its customers. Moreover, this type of reactive measure provides no information about the relative importance customers attach to the issue about which they complained. The source of dissatisfaction might be very important or relatively trivial. Reactive measures typically don't provide information about what is most important to customers.

Many of the problems that Kmart has experienced in recent years can be attributed to overreliance on reactive measures and underutilization of proactive measures of strategic health. Ask any manager of a Kmart store how they measure customer satisfaction and the typical response will be "the 800 number." Although Kmart has done a good job of facilitating customer complaints by establishing and promoting the use of its 800 number, they spend far too many resources in a reactive mode. Company-wide programs are designed and implemented to address aggregated customer complaints, with no evaluation of which concerns are most important to their targeted market. Naturally, as soon as one fire is extinguished, another flares up—resulting in the "program of the month." Is it any wonder that Kmart has been ineffective in articulating and implementing a coherent strategy?

Reactive measures, like customer complaints and defections, cannot help in identifying value opportunities, will not reveal a complete list of benefits sought by targeted customers, will not, typically, reveal the relative importance of those benefits, and are unlikely to provide information regarding competitive position. A value-driven philosophy of business requires *proactive measures* of strategic health. Simply put, proactive measures entail *actively* seeking customer definitions of value and *actively* evaluating the production of value. Reactive measures include only what is left when a proactive approach is not taken. Reactive measures lead to ambiguous direction and serendipitous accomplishments.

Chapter 5 describes the process of proactively identifying value opportunities by evaluating products/services and markets in terms of highly specific value criteria. The efficacy of these criteria, however, is dependent upon the quality of the measures employed. Reactive measures, like those described above, are likely to provide a distorted perspective of value opportunities. Proactive measures, like those described below, will help to determine effective value strategies and to evaluate the effectiveness of implementation efforts.

Critical Issues in Strategic Value Measurement

The remainder of this chapter describes procedures we have found to be effective in developing proactive measures of strategic health. Critical issues center on defining the targeted market, determining what information to collect, using that information effectively, and accounting for changes in value definition and perspective.

Who to Ask

We have already emphasized that the most important issue within the domain of value is that *value is defined by the customer*. Due to the recent emphasis on a market orientation to business, many companies already understand the importance of this issue. Unfortunately, most of these companies narrowly define the term "customer" to mean "those people who use our products and services." This myopic view of "the customer" has led many businesses into strategic ruin for two important reasons. First, customers who currently do business with your bank may not even represent the market you have targeted as a significant value

opportunity, as described in Chapter 5. Consequently, their definitions of value, while important to *them*, may prove relatively unimportant—or even misleading—to you. Second, many customers
within your targeted market may currently do business with the
competition. Their perspective on value probably differs from the
perspective of your current customers, and it is precisely those differences that must be identified. The bank that intends to capitalize fully on value opportunities must understand value as defined
by all current customers *and potential customers* of the targeted
market. This implies:

1. Identifying markets that represent value opportunities as
   discussed in Chapter 5.

2. Identifying all current customers and potential customers
   within those markets.

3. Determining how all members of the targeted market
   define value.

Moreover, care must be taken to understand market definitions of
value as they pertain to *specific products and services*. Consistent
with Value Proposition 3, discussed in Chapter 2, customers will
define their expectations of benefits related to checking accounts
very differently from their expected benefits of sound retirement
planning—and they expect the costs of each to differ as well.
Measures of strategic value, therefore, must account for those
dimensions of value defined by the value-opportunity market(s)
relative to specific product and service offerings.

What to Ask

Our work on strategic health measures with numerous clients
across several industries suggests that there are four ways of
knowing about market-defined value:

1. Tenacity Method
   - Always true before...
     (Violates Value Proposition 5)

2. Authority Method
 - Boss says it's so!
   (Violates Value Proposition 3)

3. Intuition Method
 - Stands to reason.
   (Violates Value Proposition 3)

4. Common Sense Method
 - "Ask 'em"

Unfortunately, few bank managers are willing to make the investment necessary to engage in the common sense approach, believing that they already understand the dimensions of customer value based on their collective experience. These managers pay lip service to "customer satisfaction" by designing surveys from an *internal* perspective, then asking customers for a variety of ratings on questions that may not even be relevant. The problem with this approach was clearly identified years ago by Will Rogers, when he said: *It's not always what we don't know that gives us trouble, it's what we know that ain't so.*

When you ask customers about their satisfaction with specific products or services, you must be sure to ask about the dimensions and attributes of that product or service that the customer regards as relevant. *Internal* definitions of relevant value dimensions frequently overlook important dimensions of value from the market point of view, and often include dimensions that the market considers irrelevant. Ratings of satisfaction on such measures are counterproductive as indicators of strategic health.

The methodology for determining what to ask regarding customer perceptions of value involves three steps. First, interviews or focus groups with representative members of the targeted market will help identify all issues considered relevant by that market. These issues must be translated into corresponding questions expressed in terms readily understood by that market. Second, issues must be translated into quantifiable measures using the most appropriate of various scales and delivery systems currently available, and these measures should be tested with a representative sample of the targeted market. Third, the resulting data must be analyzed to identify the specific dimensions of value considered important for this product/market, along with their related attributes. Subsequent, repeated measures of customer value will focus on the *right* questions and will provide *market-based* information on all the dimensions of value *considered relevant by the customer*.

In order to evaluate the validity of your strategic value measures you must examine the relationship between the dimensions of value as articulated by the market and their purchasing behavior or their expressions of overall satisfaction. Behavioral indicators might include customer retention rates, willingness of customers to build relationships with a bank, or the likelihood that customers will recommend the bank to others. Overall satisfaction with the bank can be assessed with a rating scale. This process of developing value measures assures the following:

- Value is defined by the customer (market).
- All relevant dimensions of customer value are measured.
- Specific attributes adequately represent value dimensions.
- Both benefit and price dimensions are included.
- Measures of customer *perceptions* of value will be both valid and reliable.

How to Use

Development of value measures and collection of value data is a necessary first step in evaluating your bank's strategic health. The collection of data alone, however, does not yield *information*. This is as true of strategic health data as it is of financial data. In order to maximize strategic health data, it must be properly utilized.

Value Proposition 1 states that "the existence and perception of value are necessary conditions in any exchange situation." This proposition implies that, for every product/market there are basic benefits at a specified price that must be provided if the bank is to even qualify as a viable supplier. Recall, if you will, the discussion of home purchases from Chapter 5. For any given market segment there exists a specific set of needs that must be met in order for homes to *qualify* for consideration. Once the couple has identified those homes that fall into the qualifying set, they will *determine* which home to buy based upon their list of *desirable* benefits. These determining needs might include such things as an extra bedroom, a garage, a fireplace, proximity to good schools, low down payment, low monthly payments, and lowest total cost.

The point of this illustration is that each of the qualifying needs, whether in terms of benefits or the price that the customer pays for those benefits, must be met if the home (or bank) is even to be part of the consideration set. Each of those qualifying needs is equally important, and all must be met in order for the product or service offering to be considered. This is a sort of "check the box" exercise: If *any* of these qualifying "boxes" are not checked, the home or bank is dropped from further consideration.

The list of determining needs is another matter entirely. Our young couple *wants* the lowest possible down payment and low monthly payments but will trade up on those criteria (to the limits of the qualifying parameter) in order to get some of the other things they want—like the extra bedroom or the fireplace. Moreover, the list of benefits in the determining category are not all of equal importance. The extra bedroom and yard space may be far more important than proximity to schools or the lowest possible monthly payment. The analysis of our value measurement data must clearly articulate these differences, both between generic and differentiating attributes (qualifying and determining needs), and differences of importance within the differentiating attributes because such differences have important implications for strategic health. Significant weaknesses relating to qualifying attributes *must* be corrected if you wish to continue as a player in a particular product/market. Significant strengths related to important determining needs can be leveraged for a sustainable value advantage.

The type of value measure described in the preceding section of this chapter will generate data suitable for examination of these differences, *but only if the analysis is focused at the product/market level, and only if the data collection is based on the proposition that value is normative,* i.e., perceptions of value are usually based on perceptions of alternatives. Analyses that *aggregate* data *across* products/markets will result in meaningless *averages,* while analyses that does include perceptions of *competitive value* will produce no information about *differentiation.*

One very simple example from discount retailing is illustrative of the type of information one can generate from quantitative data, properly collected (see Figure 6-4). The market consisted of single, female heads of households with modest income. The product line is clothing. Data analysis involved a combination of factor analysis, regression analysis, and statistical variance.

The vertical axis of Figure 6-4 represents the importance of attributes as determined by this market segment. The horizontal axis represents differences in performance across competitors as judged by those same customers, with greater differences appearing further to the right. The first five attributes are considered to be relatively important by customers, but these same customers don't see much difference in performance across the competition. These may be regarded as qualifying attributes—you must be "in the ball park" on each of these in order to be considered. The seven attributes on which competitive performance varies (those on the right side of the graph) are differentiation attributes. Some competitors are perceived to provide high levels of performance on these attributes, while others perform poorly. This market segment will make their purchase decisions based on their perceptions of how well stores perform on the most important, or on some important combination, of these attributes. The ability to analyze information in this manner is extremely useful for strategic and tactical decisions.

Figure 6-4
CATEGORIZING NEEDS: A QUANTITATIVE APPROACH

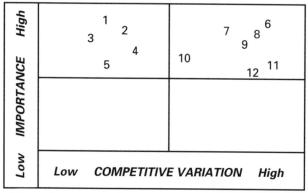

1. Good prices
2. Convenient
3. Reasonable
   return policy
4. Easy access/ exit

5. Clear weekly
   ads/ bargains
6. Courteous
   polite staff
7. Neat, clean store
8. Helpful staff

9. Good store
   design/ layout
10. Good quality
11. Large selection
12. Attractive stores

The strategic value of this type of analysis is that it provides information, from the viewpoint of the targeted market, regarding the benefits sought by that market. The analysis provides information regarding those benefits that *must* be present in order for the service provider to be considered, while also revealing the relative importance of *desired* benefits that can differentiate one competitor from another. But, in the absence of additional competitive information, the analysis tells you nothing about your *relative* strategic health.

One final example vividly illustrates the importance of strategic health as interpreted from the customer perspective (Figure 6-5). For this example we return to discount retailing within a limited geographic market. For illustrative purposes, we have limited the analysis to an examination of differentiation *dimensions* for a single, targeted product/market. The value dimensions are arranged in descending order of importance. Market perceptions of three discount retailers, Kmart, Wal-mart, and Target, are contrasted in the analysis.

Figure 6-5
COMPETITIVE PROFILE

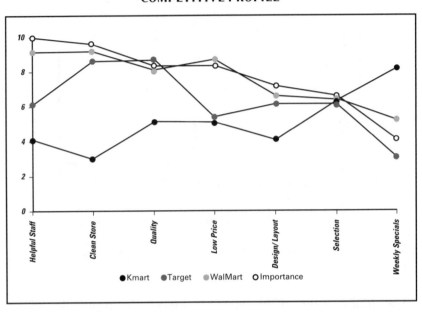

Wal-mart has clearly done the best job of identifying what's most important to this market segment and has allocated resources in such a way as to have a clear differential value advantage over Kmart. Wal-mart's strategic health in this product/market is excellent. Although Kmart has a significant strength on the dimension of "weekly specials" (including advertising), this strength is relatively unimportant to the market segment, and therefore represents a misallocation of resources. Kmart could cut costs in this area with no negative effect on its strategic health. Moreover, the additional cash could be redirected to training in the important areas of staff helpfulness and store cleanliness.

Note that this analysis does not *explicitly* evaluate strategic health in terms of the value equation as presented earlier in this book. To do so requires *separating* benefits from the perceived price of those benefits, and analyzing the former in terms of the latter. We believe the implications of such an analysis to be so powerful that we have devoted the entire next chapter to the use of strategic value measurement data in the context of a value matrix.

When to Measure

One final note regarding the customer perspective on strategic health: **Customer definitions of value change over time.** Customer satisfaction with value delivery is a function of their *expectations relative to their perceptions* of your bank's performance on both the price and benefit dimensions. We've already demonstrated the importance of collecting market *perceptions* of value delivery because those perceptions are the only reality for the customer. We've also emphasized the importance of having the *customer* define the dimensions of value that are important at a particular point in time. But these dimensions of value, and the related expectations for each dimension, are not static. Value Proposition 5 holds that value definitions and perceptions change over time because market expectations are driven by a constantly evolving operating environment.

Examples of change—competitive, technological, social, and regulatory—are discussed throughout this book. Each type of change brings with it changes in market expectations, indeed, changes in the very dimensions customers use to define value for a product or service. An effective system of customer value measurement will capture changing market expectations, and will do so in a proactive manner.

The obvious implication of Value Proposition 6 is that customer value perceptions must be measured on a periodic and regular basis. Analysis, such as those described earlier and in the next chapter, will provide information regarding changing perceptions of relative value delivered. Less obvious is the fact that the very dimensions used by the market to define value may change over time. Two simple procedures will help to assure that customer value measures become dynamic rather than remain static.

First, value measures should enable and encourage open-ended customer comments. These open-ended comments must be systematically analyzed on a periodic basis, using the techniques of content analysis. This approach will help to identify new issues

123

of importance to the market that can subsequently be evaluated quantitatively.

Second, a systematic program of focus group interviews will aid in identifying emerging issues of importance within targeted products/markets. Recall that the development of customer value measures began with such focus group interviews for the purpose of identifying potential dimensions of customer value. An ongoing program of focus group interviews will, similarly, aid in the identification of new ways in which customers think about value.

As new issues are identified, whether through content analysis of customer comments or through focus groups, pilot questions can be included in the ongoing measurement program. A periodic re-evaluation of value dimensions through factor analysis will assist in determining whether these new attributes of value simply constitute new levels of expectation on existing dimensions of value, or define entirely new dimensions of value not previously measured. This approach to customer value measurement assures that your measures are proactive and dynamic, constantly capturing perceptions of value even as value expectations change.

The customer perspective on value or, more precisely, the market perspective on value serves as the most important indicator of strategic health. Banks that evaluate strategic health solely from an internal or shareholder perspective will likely go the way of the dinosaur—and we have seen ample evidence of that during the last two decades. Important as internal perspectives on quality and shareholder perspectives on financial health may be, if they are not driven by customer perspectives on value, they will provide only serendipitous success. Many banks that have looked for success through various quality initiatives have learned this lesson the hard way, continually improving the quality of products and services without determining first whether these are even the products and services most valued by the market. Quality, like all benefit dimensions of value, is defined by the market.

SUMMARY

The shift to a value paradigm requires new thinking about appropriate measures of value performance. Any change of business orientation that is not accompanied by changes in the measurement of performance will result in no change at all. Measures of financial health can only tell you where you've been. They reveal nothing about where you are going. To get a view through the windshield rather than through the rear-view mirror requires measures of strategic health.

We have identified several critical issues relative to the design and use of strategic value measures. The key principles regarding strategic value measurement are:

1. Value is defined from the customer's perspective.

2. Value measures must distinguish between qualifying and determining dimensions of value.

3. Value measures must reveal the relative importance of differentiating attributes for efficient and effective resource allocation.

4. Value data must be disaggregated to the product/market level.

5. Value measures must be sufficiently flexible to capture changing market definitions of value.

The design and implementation of appropriate strategic value measures will enable you to evaluate your bank's strategic health *relative to that of the competition*. The use of value measurement data in the value matrix, described in the next chapter, will enable you to determine your value position from a market perspective and will lead to improvements in your value delivery system, described in Chapter 8.

Endnotes

1. Treece, James B (1994) "A Bank Boss at the Brink," *Business Week* (September 19).

2. Zeithaml, Valerie A., A. Parasuraman, and Leonard I. Berry (1990) *Delivering Quality Service: Balancing Customer Expectations and Perceptions.* New York: The Free Press.

3. Stata, Ray (1989) "Organizational Learning—The Key to Management Innovation," *Sloan Management Review* (Spring), pp. 63–74.

4. May 1990 Report, American Banking Association.

7. THE VALUE MATRIX

> "Why would I pay $6.00 for crappy service when I can get it from my bank for $2.00?"
> -Mrs. Lefkowitz

Value Proposition 3 points out that value opportunities are embedded within the different product/markets that your bank serves. Further, as the chapter on the Product/Market Matrix makes clear (Chapter 5), not all product/markets will render value opportunities of the same magnitude or importance. It is essential that the bank examine the different product/markets in terms of their capacity to produce a differential value advantage that will translate into superior performance. To do this we have developed two tools, the Value Matrix and the Vulnerability Index. These tools are designed specifically to: (1) identify potential value opportunities, (2) to identify the means for achieving them, (3) to point out those value attributes on which your bank is vulnerable, and (4) to identify your competition's points of vulnerability. Knowing this information will permit your bank to develop stronger customer retention programs and to develop stronger as well as more focused customer acquisition programs.

THE VALUE MATRIX

Recall, if you will, that we have defined value in exchange as the ratio between an important customer benefit and the price that the customer pays for that benefit. In other words:

VALUE = BENEFIT/PRICE

Benefits are specific to each product/market and have to be identified. The chapter on strategic measurement pointed out the who, what, where, and how these benefits are identified. The more specifically these benefits can be identified the more focused will be your value analysis resulting in a more effective subsequent implementation effort. For example, a global benefit such as customer service will be of less use to your analysis than will specific information on what exactly your product/market believes is customer service. Does customer service mean no waiting, or speedy response to your inquiries, or easy access to bank personnel? More specifically, what does no waiting actually mean? What do customers in the product/market mean by speedy response to their inquiries or easy access to bank personnel? The point is don't be satisfied with a global definition of customer benefits. The more specifically these benefits are defined, the more potent and useful will be your analysis and subsequent strategic decisions.

Another point to keep in mind is that some customer benefits will be more important than others. Trying to develop and implement a value strategy based on relatively unimportant customer benefits is a sure fire formula for failure. Value is directly linked to the relative importance of customer benefits.

Price or customer cost can be conceptualized in several different ways. First, there is the intrinsic cost of a service. This is represented by the fee or the rate charged by the bank. This fee or rate also has a relative component to it. It is relative to the fees or rates of your competitors. Second, there is a price or customer cost that the customer pays in terms of hassle or effort to transact with your bank. Not only do they have to pay a dollar fee for a service but they also have to expend time driving, looking for a parking space, getting problems solved, waiting in line, and a number of other time-absorbing activities. These customer costs typically reduce the perceived benefit portion of the value equation.

If we align the two components of value in a matrix, similar to the one shown in Figure 7-1, we can construct a Value Matrix. This Value Matrix in Figure 7-1 is constructed from survey information obtained in a commercial bank market. The benefit attribute arrayed on the horizontal axis is the "ability of the bank to solve my financial service problems." It was the most important attribute identified in this market and the number one attribute mentioned in terms of staying with a specific bank. The scores on this benefit attribute were collected in a market survey using a five point scale ranging from "very good" to "very bad." A score of 5 meant that the customer perceived his or her bank to be very good at solving his or her financial service problems. Conversely, a score of 1 meant that the bank was doing a very poor job of solving his or her financial services problems.

Figure 7-1
THE VALUE MATRIX

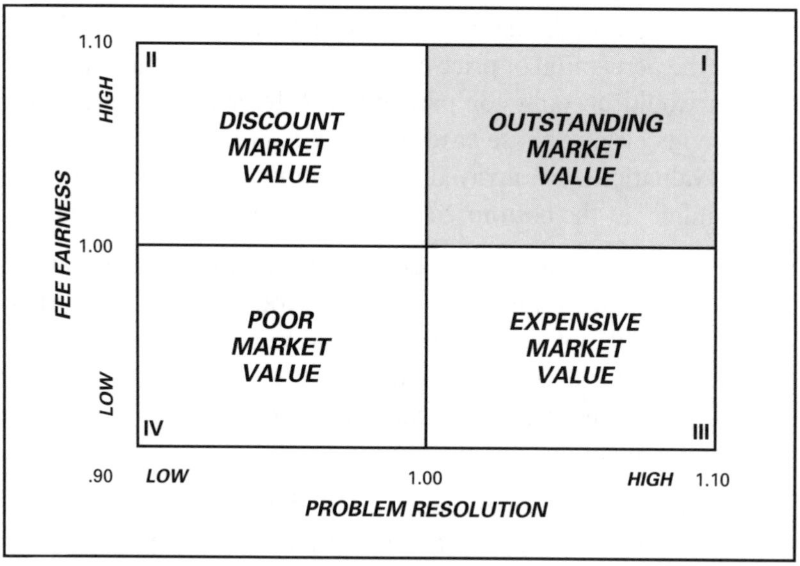

In addition, we obtained importance scores on the different attributes. In using the Value Matrix, the importance score serves as a screening variable that allows the prioritization of various benefits for future analysis. As mentioned previously, "problem resolution" is the benefit attribute that scored the highest in importance. Importance is measured in a similar fashion to attribute performance with a 5—meaning "very important" and a 1 meaning "very unimportant."

Price was operationalized by asking bank customers to rate the fairness of the fee and rate structure at their bank, *relative to the fees and rates charged by other banks*. This relativity is extremely important. Failure to measure these attributes in terms of their relative market performance renders the analysis myopic and too focused on a single bank. A score of 5 meant that they thought the fee structure was "very fair" while a score of 1 meant that they thought the fee structure was "very unfair." This measurement of price is, of course, perceptual in nature and accommodates the importance of Value Proposition 1. In addition, it reflects a perception of the relative nature of price in the marketplace. This is important because while some banks may charge the same rates or even have a highly similar rate structure, other factors influencing the perception of price can also come into play. Those other factors would account for perceptual differences between price evaluations even in those cases where no actual difference exists. Price evaluations are arrayed on the vertical axis ranging from "very unfair" at the bottom, to "very fair" at the top of the matrix.

In measuring these attributes, do not be surprised to find that the range of responses varies from "very good" to "average." Most customers will not stay with their bank if they think that its ability to provide a very important attribute is "bad" or "very bad." Typically, this restriction of range is found in most surveys of customer perceptions of value.

Each bank will have a score on both the "problem resolution" benefit attribute and the price perception. If we aggregate all of these scores we get a market score for each measure. This can be interpreted as the "average score" for each attribute item. Thus, we will get an average score for the "problem resolution" attribute and an average score for the "fee fairness" measure. If we divide the average market score for the benefit attribute into each bank's benefit attribute score, the scale now is translated into a range of scores centered on 1.0, the market average. Thus, all scores are now expressed in terms of the market. The actual range of the individual bank scores will depend upon customer perceptions. This same translation is done for the price variable, with again the same market average of 1.0 resulting.

Two pieces of important information are now made available in the Value Matrix. First, a bank that scores .8 on the benefit attribute falls 20 percent below market average. Similarly, a bank that scores 1.10 is perceived to be 10 percent higher than average on that attribute. Thus, value can be expressed in terms of an overall market average. Second, the difference between individual banks can also be interpreted. For example, a bank scoring 1.0 (average) on the benefit attribute is doing 20 percent better than the bank that scores .8.

Outstanding Market Value Positions

The intersection of the average attribute scores (1.0, 1.0) permits the division of the Value Matrix into four meaningful and market relevant quadrants. The upper right-hand quadrant is labeled the "outstanding value" quadrant corresponding to ratings on both the benefit attribute and the price attribute that are above average. A bank positioned in this quadrant is one that scores high on the "problem resolution" attribute and high (towards the "very fair" end) on the price measure (fee fairness). This tells us that any bank positioned within this quadrant is delivering outstanding customer value as defined by their customers. They are doing a very good job in providing a very important benefit at a price that is perceived to be very fair. They are providing outstanding value to their customers. Mere inclusion within this quadrant does not imply equal absolute value. The outstanding value quadrant has its own hierarchical positions, with those banks closer to the upper right-hand corner providing the greatest value.

Discount Market Value Positions

The upper left-hand quadrant is designated as the "discount market value" quadrant. Banks positioned in this quadrant score high on the price measure (high fee fairness), but below market average in their ability to deliver on the benefit attribute (problem resolution). In other words, customers of these banks are receiving below average benefits, but are paying a lower price for them. Relative to the banks positioned in the "outstanding value" quadrant, these banks are providing a secondary level of value. Only these two quadrants define actual value positions. The other two quadrants describe banks with product/service offerings of lesser value.

Poor Market Value Positions

Those banks positioned in the lower left-hand quadrant are providing poor market value. Banks positioned within this "poor market value" quadrant are providing below average delivery on the benefit attribute and at a high customer price (low scores on the fee fairness measure). This is the worst value position. These banks find their management of customer value is out of whack. They are particularly vulnerable to customer acquisition efforts of better positioned banks. A bank positioned in this quadrant will find itself in an extremely untenable position.

Expensive Market Value Positions

Finally, those banks positioned in the "expensive market value" quadrant (lower right-hand of the matrix) are those banks that are generating above average scores on the benefit attribute, but are also perceived as being high priced. Customers are getting good benefit, but they are paying for it. This is a low value quadrant, but relative to the "poor market value" bank, this position is more tenable.

Analyzing Value Positions

Banks in the "outstanding market value" quadrant are the least susceptible to competitive pressures. Their customers are receiving outstanding value in their banking relationship. Banks in the "discount market value" quadrant are more susceptible to competitive efforts on the part of banks that can deliver greater benefit at the same perceived customer price. If the perceived customer price is the same, customers will maximize their utility and value by choosing a greater value delivering bank. Banks in the "expensive market value" are susceptible to competitive pressures based on a price advantage. Customer value can be increased by offering the same level of benefit, but at a lower perceived price. Finally, those banks in the "poor market value" quadrant are susceptible to acquisitive actions based on both increased benefit and decreased price.

This is a general explanation of how the value matrix works. Let's take a specific look at an actual market situation where seven banks are competing for customers.

OPERATIONALIZING THE VALUE MATRIX

The value matrix in Figure 7-2 reflects the perceptions of 400 bank customers in a market with a population of about 50,000. There are seven banks in this market. Two are small independents, four are branches of large holding companies, and one is a large statewide former S&L headquartered in this area.

The customers who responded to the survey were all customers of one or more of the banks involved. Customers' use of a specific institution was determined by asking respondents to identify the bank they considered to be their primary financial institution. Customers were asked to rate their bank on a number of benefit attributes identified earlier in a series of focus groups held in this market area. They were then asked to rate the importance of the benefit attributes in their decision to remain as customers of the bank. Two benefit attributes emerged from the importance screening: (1) "The ability of the bank to solve my financial service problems," and (2) "The ability of the bank to provide me with the kind of service I need." For the sake of explication, we will focus on the first benefit attribute as the utility dimension of the value equation. In addition, respondents were asked to rate their perception of the fairness of the fee and rate structure offered by their bank. "Fee fairness" is the price dimension of the value equation.

Figure 7-2
VALUE POSITIONS FOR SEVEN BANKS

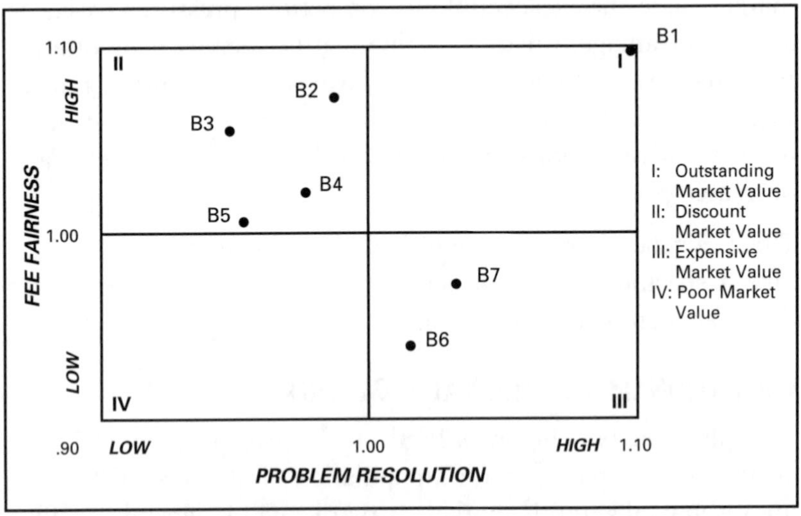

By arraying "problem resolution" on the horizontal axis and "fee fairness" on the vertical axis of the matrix and using the approach outlined earlier to delineate value positions on the matrix, we get the situation portrayed in Figure 7-2. Bank 1 is the only bank located in the "outstanding market value" quadrant of the matrix. It is the clear value leader in this market. Four banks are positioned by their customers in the "discount market value" quadrant, Banks 2, 3, 4, and 5. Banks 2, 3, and 4, according to their customers, are providing below average delivery on the "problem resolution" attribute, but are doing so at a perceived level of cost that is fair. The tradeoff between lower performance on the important benefit attribute, and the fairness of the price they are paying for the benefit, creates a lower type of value proposition. Bank 3 is the other locally owned independent, while Banks 2 and 4 are two branches of two large holding companies. Bank 5, the converted S&L, is precariously perched on the boundary of the "poor market value" quadrant. Their position is a function of customer perceptions that indicate their fee structure is only average, but their ability to deliver on the "problem resolution" benefit attribute is below average. Any negative change in customer perceptions of fee structure could tip them into the "poor market value" quadrant. This is a dangerous position for them, especially given the need for increased fee income. They can only increase fees at the risk of damaging an already bad value perception. Two banks occupy the "expensive market value" quadrant. Banks 6 and 7 are branches of two of the states largest holding companies. Their customers perceive that they are receiving above average benefit, but are paying higher fees for that benefit.

By examining all of the relative positions of the banks on the value matrix, strategic implications become clear. For example, Banks 2, 3, and 4 can improve their value positions by improving their ability to solve their customers' financial service problems. Their fee and rate structures are perceived to be fair, but their customers do not rate their ability to solve their financial service problems very highly.

Bank 5 has a double problem. Their customers do not perceive their fee structure to be necessarily fair, but rather average. This is interesting and points out the perceptual nature of price. This bank offers its customers free checking and has the lowest mortgage rates in the market. However, they are also known for two other factors that could adversely affect the price perception. First, their customers indicate that the bank offers the lowest level of customer service in the market. This affects the intangible component of price. It is very difficult to do business with this bank. Second, they have instituted a pricing policy that attaches fees to every product/service offering or transaction. While free checking is used as a loss leader and relationship builder, customers find that they are paying for this relationship. Perhaps more importantly, their ability to deliver on the important attribute of problem resolution is perceived as very low by their customers. Only one other bank, Bank 3, has a lower rating. This coincides with their low customer service ratings obtained independently.

Clearly, Bank 1 has established a differential value advantage. Customers rate Bank 1 extremely high on the two components that create customer value in this market. They are seen as the top bank in terms of their ability to solve customers financial service problems, and are seen as the bank that has the fairest fee and rate structure in the market.

How does this affect their performance? Bank 1 generates the top ROA in the market and has the strongest customer retention track record. In addition to data on customer perceptions of benefits and price, information was collected on their willingness to switch banks. Bank 1 was the most often cited bank as the bank to which customers intended to switch when, and if, they ended their relationship with their current bank. Moreover, every customer at every bank, except Bank 1, indicated a bank they would be willing to switch to. In the case of Bank 1 customers, only 50 percent indicated a targeted bank. The other 50 percent said they would not be willing to switch. Bank 1 has leveraged its differential value advantage into a strong customer retention program that, in turn, has proven very profitable for them.

THE VULNERABILITY INDEX

The Vulnerability Index, when used in conjunction with the Value Matrix, provides even greater insight into the competitive positioning of the seven banks. A Vulnerability Index based on the information used to compile the Value Matrix is shown in Table 7-1. The two most important benefit attributes in bank customer retention are shown at the top of the table. These are the level of customer service and problem resolution. The columns headed Ics and Ips represent the importance scores for each benefit attribute for each bank. Again, these are customer driven. The scale used to generate these scores was a 5-point scale, ranging from "very important" (5) to "very unimportant" (1). The columns headed Rcs and Rps represent the attribute score for customer service and problem resolution respectively. These too were measured using a 5-point scale with 5 meaning "very good" and 1 meaning "very poor." The importance score represents a weight given to the benefit attribute score. In the Value Matrix we used the importance score to screen those benefit attributes that were most important. Here we will multiply the importance score by the benefit attribute score to get a weighted score. These weighted scores are shown under the columns headed Tcs and Tps respectively. The maximum score that can be attained for these two benefit attributes would be 50, (5 x 5) for each of the two attribute-importance contribution. If we had three attribute-importance combinations, the total score would be 75, or (5 x 5) for each of the three combinations.

Table 7-1
CALCULATION OF VULNERABILITY INDEX FOR
RETAIL BANK COMPETITORS

	CUSTOMER SERVICE			PROBLEM SOLUTION			VULNERABILITY INDEX
	I^1_{cs} * R^2_{cs} = T^3_{cs}			I^4_{ps} * R^5_{ps} = T^6_{ps}			$(T_{cs} + T_{ps}/50)$
Bank 1	4.77	4.64	22.13	4.82	4.64	22.36	.89
Bank 2	4.44	4.39	19.49	4.78	4.28	20.46	.80
Bank 3	4.44	4.25	18.87	4.56	4.19	19.11	.76
Bank 4	4.55	4.33	19.70	4.58	4.36	19.97	.79
Bank 5	4.48	4.29	19.22	4.45	4.10	18.25	.75
Bank 6	4.47	4.47	19.98	4.31	4.09	17.63	.75
Bank 7	4.52	4.17	18.85	4.52	4.52	20.43	.79

[1]Importance of Customer Service
[2]Rating of Customer Service
[3]Total Customer Service Score
[4]Importance of Problem Solution
[5]Rating of Problem Solving
[6]Total Problem Solution Score

In the current two attribute case, the index is calculated by dividing the summated scores for the two attribute-importance combinations, and then dividing that score by 50. This puts the index on a scale of 0 to 1.0. The higher the index the lower the vulnerability.

Referring again to Table 7-1 shows that Bank 1 is the least vulnerable. It has a Vulnerability Index of .89. Bank 2 is somewhat more vulnerable with an index of .8, followed by Bank 4 and Bank 7 (.79), Bank 3 (.76), and Banks 5 and 6 (.75). The logic of the Vulnerability Index is readily apparent from the calculation of the index. In interpreting the individual importance and attribute rating scores, a score of 4.5 or greater is typically interpreted as "very important" and "very good," respectively. Scores greater than 3.5, but less than 4.49 are interpreted as "important" or "good." Using this interpretation, Bank 1 scores "very good" on both customer service and problem solution which were rated very important by the customers of Bank 1. These customers are telling us that on those benefit attributes that they consider the most important, their bank is doing a very good job.

To see why Bank 4 is more vulnerable, look at the importance scores for the two benefit attributes. Both were rated very important by their customers, but customers reported that Bank 4 was doing merely a good job. This difference between importance rating and attribute score can be thought of as a "value void" we discussed in Chapter 5. The greater the difference between the importance score and the evaluation of that attribute, the greater the vulnerability that bank has on that benefit attribute. The difference between the two Vulnerability Index scores is called a "vulnerability differential."

Keep in mind that since the importance score and the benefit attribute rating are measuring different things, you must resist the temptation to treat differences in absolute terms. Rather, value gaps have to be looked at in categorical terms, using the breakdowns of very important/important and very good/good. The

Vulnerability Index provides a global measure of the bank's relative vulnerability and decomposing the index into its constituent parts.

Points of vulnerability can be identified for several of the banks in this market. First, let's make the point that Bank 1 is least vulnerable. Note that this coincides with its differential value advantage shown in the Value Matrix and is one of the benefits accruing from a differential value advantage. Moreover, it explains why it has the best customer retention record and why it is the most mentioned second choice bank in the market. Simply put, it is providing the most value as determined by customers in this market.

Bank 2, on the other hand, is somewhat vulnerable based on its problem solution score. Bank 2 customers rated this benefit attribute very important, but it is only doing a good job satisfying this attribute. A bank wishing to increase its market share would find Bank 2 vulnerable on this point. Keep in minds, "good" does not cut it anymore!

Bank 3 is most vulnerable on the problem solution attribute because of the gap between the importance of the attribute and the customer rating of the bank. Note, however, that the customer service attribute is not as important to these customers as to other customers. Note also that they rate their bank "good" on an "important" attribute. This would suggest that Bank 3 would be less vulnerable on this value attribute.

Bank 4 is vulnerable on both attributes, as is Bank 5. Bank 6 is less vulnerable because these two attributes are not as important to their customers. Finally, Bank 7 is vulnerable on the problem solution attribute.

Clearly for Bank 1, customer acquisition at the expense of its competitors is viable. They can focus their promotion targeting customers of competing banks. Similarly, customer acquisition at the expense of Bank 1 will be very difficult.

Identifying Value Differentials in Customer Groups

One of the benefits of the Value Matrix is its ability to decompose customer groups to identify which segments are perceiving value and which ones are not. Let's take a look at the difference in value perceptions that exist between male and female clients.

Women—A Neglected Value Opportunity

In 65 percent of the households surveyed in this market, the woman is the individual who is in charge of banking tasks. She is the individual who makes the deposits, cashes checks, checks on statement errors, and perhaps most importantly, has a significant say about the continuance of the banking relationship.

Moreover, across the United States, women are becoming an increasingly important segment of the financial services market. Consider, if you will, the results of a recent study of 4,500 women conducted by *Working Women* magazine concerning how women handle their money.[1]

- More than 70 percent of the respondents indicate that they can afford to invest, while half are already active investors.

- Twenty-eight percent of investing women invest in stocks or stock funds. Most, however, choose less risky investments such as passbook savings or CDs.

- Twenty-one percent indicated that they did not really know enough about alternative investment vehicles to invest.

- Nearly 46 percent indicated that they feel more confident about investing if they had clearer explanations of investing in pamphlets and articles, while 38 percent were looking for an advisor they could trust. Finally, 11 percent pointed out that they were looking for a more helpful attitude and personal service from financial counselors.

- One respondent summed up the lack of service that women receive from the financial service industry by saying the following: "It would be nice if the financial services industry, which is run mostly by men, understood that women are interested in their advice but want to be treated with respect and spoken to in plain English."

In short, the survey indicates that there is a huge pent-up demand for the competitors that can provide the level of service and value that these women demand. This is an extremely important segment for the financial services industry and, as the study points out, an extremely neglected segment. It represents fertile ground for long-term value-centered banking relationships.

If we examine the seven banks identified earlier in the study to see which of the banks are positioned to leverage this segment we will see a situation not dissimilar to many commercial banking markets around the country. The Value Matrix shown in Figure 7-3 captures mens' and womens' perceptions of the value they are receiving from their own banks. This Value Matrix utilizes "level of customer service" as the utility attribute. This was done because "level of customer service" was rated as very important by both segments. "Fee fairness" is used, as was the earlier case, as the price component of the value equation. Only those customers who indicated that they had a multiple product/service relationship with their bank, including CDs, comprised this respondent group.

We've located the different banks onto the Value Matrix using the same approach discussed earlier. The banks are identified with a numerical subscript and the respondent group is identified with either a M (male) or F (female) subscript. Thus, B1F would represent Bank 1's female customers' perceptions.

In the "Outstanding Value Quadrant," Bank 1 and Bank 2 are the only banks that are perceived by their female clients to be delivering outstanding value. Women customers feel as though they are getting above average customer service at a fair fee. This combination creates a solid value perception. Again, Bank 1 was identified earlier as the top value deliverer in the market. Bank 2, it will be recalled, was positioned in the "Discount Value Quadrant." Only two other customer groups, both male, were located in this quadrant. Male customers at Banks 3 and 4 can be found in the "Outstanding Value Quadrant."

Figure 7-3

VALUE POSITIONS: MALES (M) VERSUS FEMALES (F)

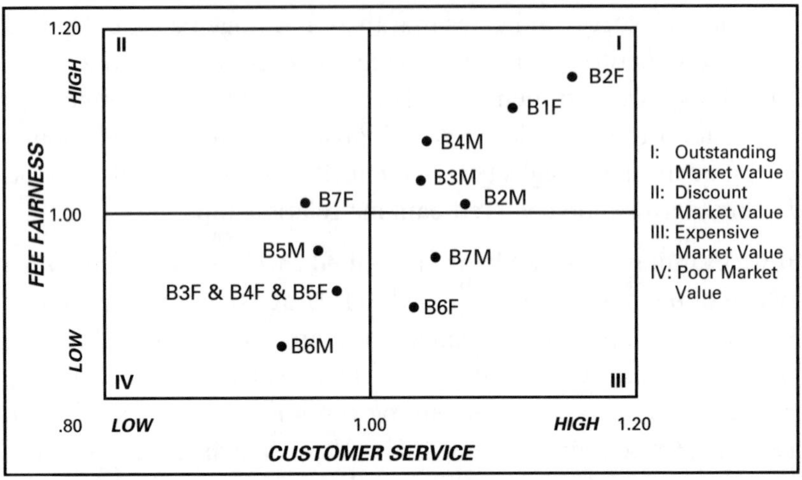

Perhaps most interesting in this analysis is the number of banks located in the "Poor Market Value Quadrant" according to women customers. Women at Banks 3, 4, and 5 indicate that they are receiving below average customer service and paying a high fee for it. In addition, women at Bank 7 position their bank on the "Poor Market Value" cusp. Women at Bank 6 indicate that they are receiving above average customer service but feel as though they are paying higher fees. This locates Bank 6 in the "Expensive Value Quadrant."

This analysis has significant consequences for those banks attempting to increase their share of the investment market. Women complain about lack of respect and an unwillingness of financial services people to explain investment alternatives to them. Which of the banks is in the best position to retain customers and build those all important banking relationships that lead to increased profitability? Which of the banks in this market are positioned to leverage increased business in this segment? Who will women turn to when they are ready to invest? Clearly, according to the perceptions of women customers, only Banks 1 and 2 are perceived capable of providing them with the value they want and expect from an investment relationship. Moreover, the differential value advantage that Banks 1 and 2 have established over their competitors is significant. No other banks in the market are positioned to cash in on this potentially lucrative segment. Banks 3, 4, and 5 and, to a lesser extent, Bank 7 are vulnerable to the competitive efforts of Banks 1 and 2 to acquire female customers. To date, no such initiatives are underway.

Black and White Differentials

Another extremely important customer segment for commercial bankers is the black banking customer. Much of the recent regulation is aimed at insuring that no community sectors in which a commercial bank operates is neglected. Regulators are concerned that minority groups are well served and are served at a price that is congruent with majority segments. At the heart of the regulation is what we would clearly identify as a value question. Are minority groups receiving the same value in exchange as their majority counterparts?

Again, the Value Matrix can be very helpful in examining the perceptions of the two groups of customers. We provide just such an example using the Value Matrix shown in Figure 7-4.

The Value Matrix in Figure 7-4 depicts perceptions of black and white checking account customers to the level of customer service they are receiving and the fairness of the fees that they are charged at their respective banks. The Value Matrix has been constructed using the same rules as the previous two. Examining the perceptions mapped onto the Value Matrix provides some very interesting insights into the value gaps existing between black customers and white customers.

First, only one black customer group perceives that they are receiving outstanding market value from their institution. Bank 5 is located in the "Outstanding Market Value" quadrant. All other banks that are positioned within this quadrant are done so by their white customers. White customers at Banks 1, 2, 4, and 6 feel that they are receiving outstanding value from their checking relationship.

Minority customers at Bank 4 indicate that they are receiving below average customer service but are paying a fair fee for the service. This locates Bank 4 in the "Discount Value" quadrant. They are the only bank positioned in this area. All told, only two minority customer groups (Banks 4 and 5) indicate that they are receiving some degree of positive value in their checking account relationship.

Figure 7-4
VALUE POSITIONS: BLACK (B) VERSUS WHITE (W)

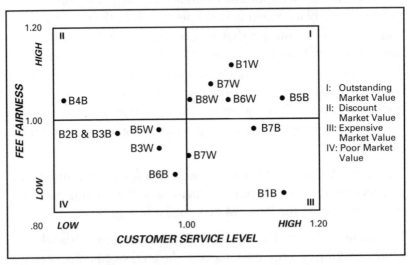

In the "Poor Market Value" quadrant, five banks are located. These include Banks 2, 3, 5, 6, and 7. Minority customers of Banks 2, 3, and 6 indicate that they are receiving poor value in their checking relationship. That is, they feel that they are receiving below average market service, and are paying a higher than average market fee for that service. Also located within this quadrant are three groups of white customers. They are customers of Banks 3, 5, and 7.

Finally, in the "Expensive Market Value" quadrant, two banks are located, banks 1 and 7. Both of these Banks are positioned in this quadrant by their minority customers.

144

What is interesting to these banks, especially from a CRA stand-point, is the differences within banks regarding perceptions of value. For example, white customers at Bank 1 indicated that they were receiving outstanding market value, while their minority counterparts felt that they were receiving only expensive market value. White customers of Bank 1 felt that they were receiving above average customer service and paying a fair fee for it, while the minority customers of Bank 1 indicated that they were receiving above average customer service but were paying an unfair fee for it. White customers at Banks 2 and 6 positioned their bank in the "Outstanding Market Value" quadrant, while minority customers at these same banks indicated that they were receiving poor market value. This comparison is most striking because of the perceptual difference in both value attributes. Minority customers at Banks 2 and 6 said they were receiving below average customer service and paying a fee that they felt was unfair for the service, while their white counterparts felt that they were receiving above average levels of customer service and paying a fair fee for it.

There are a number of other possible comparisons. The point is, these comparisons indicate that value perceptions are product/ market specific. In this case, the comparisons provide useful input into potential CRA compliance issues. Why are there differences in perceptions? What is causing these perceptual differences? How can we, as a financial services institution, increase the perceived value we are delivering to the different customer groups?

Bank 5, and to a lesser extent Bank 4, are delivering what their minority customers perceive as value in their checking relationship. This is solid information that needs to be tucked away in their CRA file for the inevitable CRA audit.

These analyses of various opportunities have demonstrated the use of two basic value oriented tools that we have designed. The Value Matrix has demonstrated a number of value propositions we outlined earlier. Essentially, the matrix indicates that value perceptions are product/market specific, and that not all banks will be able to identify, create, and service value opportunities that exist. The Vulnerability Index, when used in conjunction with the Value Matrix, identifies those points of value vulnerability that exist for a specific bank. Addressing these points of vulnerability is a must in today's competitive banking environment.

SOME CONCLUDING COMMENTS

This chapter has explicated and demonstrated two value tools that permit the examination of value opportunities within any specific product/market. We examined a market in which one bank had established a clear differential value advantage, and how that advantage was leveraged into greater customer retention and profitability. In addition, we demonstrated how the Vulnerability Index could be used to examine our own bank's exposure on value, and how to analyze competitor weaknesses. Finally, the Value Matrix was used to look at an actual situation concerning a highly neglected segment, the female customer, and the value differentials that exist between black and white customers. This type of analysis can be employed within any specific product/market to identify where value opportunities exist.

Endnotes

1. Willis, Clint (1994) "The Working Woman Money Survey," *Working Woman* (September), pp. 29-31.

8. THE VALUE DELIVERY SYSTEM: VALUE MAPPING

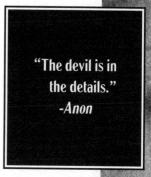

"The devil is in the details."

-Anon

The value matrix described in the preceding chapter enables bank management to evaluate its competitive value position in terms of benefit and price dimensions as defined and perceived by the market. The chapter on Strategic Value Measurement (Chapter 6) described a comprehensive approach to acquiring the market perspective on value. The efficacy of the value matrix is clearly dependent upon the rigor with which the customer perspective was obtained. Evaluation of your competitive value position for each product/market leads to two questions:

1. How can you leverage your value strengths?

2. How can you eliminate your value vulnerabilities?

The answer to either question is dependent upon your ability to identify places along your *value delivery system* that can either enhance important benefits or reduce the price that the customer pays for those benefits, or both.

To increase customer perceptions of value it is essential to evaluate your delivery of value to the customer by assessing the *entire value delivery system* for a specific product or service. It is critical to pay particular attention to those dimensions of value regarded as important by the market. This process of evaluation begins with the customer's perspective of the entire service experience and maps or charts all activities relating to critical customer interfaces with a specific product. This we call adding value for the customer and has the purpose of improving perceived benefits on important dimensions of value and/or reducing the perceived price of those benefits.

THE RATIONALE FOR VALUE MAPPING

The bank's value delivery system is essentially a *process* by which value is provided to the customer through a series of direct customer interactions and supporting activities. From the customer's point of view the *functional areas* of the bank are, or should be, transparent. Customers have little, if any, interest in what functions have to be performed in order for a check to be cashed or a mortgage processed. All they care about is that whatever cross-functional process that has to be performed is done in a manner that is quick, responsive, and hassle free. Consequently, a comprehensive evaluation of the delivery system must include all steps in the total process of providing value. Evaluations on a departmental or functional basis cannot capture the entire process, or the interfunctional linkages required for enhanced value delivery.

Many of the steps in the process of delivering value are carried out by support personnel. These "back-room" activities typically involve little or no direct contact with external customers. Designing and evaluating a *value map* helps to build a shared and consistent perception of the customer's experience with the bank for all employees and managers.

Customer perspectives on critical product/service interfaces with the bank frequently differ from those of bank employees. When a potential customer calls for information, tries to schedule an appointment, or uses an ATM, he or she is experiencing a "moment of truth" with the bank which will influence his or her perception of the entire bank. It is important, therefore, to identify all such moments of truth for each product or service and to understand the customer's perspective of the experience.

A comprehensive map of the value delivery system will identify all activities and activity interfaces relating to the delivery of value. Specifically, a *value map* will allow you to identify all activity-based service costs that can then be evaluated relative to the benefits they are designed to provide. This evaluation can lead to identifying opportunities for improving the effectiveness of the value delivery system, either by improving the benefits delivered or by reducing the costs of providing benefits that can then be translated into price reductions.

Finally, any redesign of the value delivery system will be recorded on the value map. This map can serve as a blueprint for designing control measures of quality and cost, as well as other critical aspects of performance.

Value Mapping begins with Market Perspective . . .

The analysis of a bank's value delivery system necessarily requires understanding of the market's perspective on value. Chapter 5 detailed a process for identifying product/market opportunities. In so doing it posed a number of critical questions. What are the product or service benefits considered important by the targeted market? How does the market perceive the costs of those benefits? How does your value delivery compare with that of the competition from the market's perspective? The answers to these questions provide the focus for value delivery analysis.

Consider the case of a regional bank that identified mortgage initiation and servicing (product) for first-time home buyers (market) as a significant value opportunity. Following procedures outlined in Chapter 6, the bank identified the following as benefit dimensions and constituent attributes considered important to this product/market (Figure 8-1):

Figure 8-1
VALUE DIMENSIONS AND ATTRIBUTES
Mortgages/First-Time Buyers

RELIABILITY → Does what it says → Dependable → Right the first time	**COURTESY** → Friendly staff → Showed respect → Willing to help
RESPONSIVENESS → Answered questions quickly → Kept me informed → Flexible	**CREDIBILITY** → Trustworthy → Believable → Honest
COMPETENCE → Knew products well → Good support people → Provided answers, not guesses	**UNDERSTANDING** → Listened to my needs → Understood my unique circumstances → Empathized with my frustrations
ACCESSIBILITY → Convenient hours → Easy to reach by phone → No waiting for appointments	**COMMUNICATIONS** → Explained terms and conditions clearly → Didn't talk down to me

The bank proceeded with an evaluation of benefit dimensions to distinguish between qualifying and determining dimensions. The result of that analysis indicates that lending institutions *must* demonstrate credibility, reliability, and competence in order to be considered by this market. These are the qualifying needs (Figure 8-2).

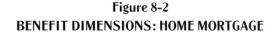

Figure 8-2
BENEFIT DIMENSIONS: HOME MORTGAGE

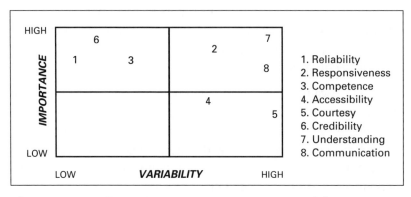

The remaining dimensions, responsiveness, accessibility, courtesy, understanding, and communication, served to differentiate among the competition, with "understanding" being the most important determining dimension for this market, and courtesy being the least important (Figure 8-3).

Figure 8-3
DETERMINING DIMENSIONS OF IMPORTANCE

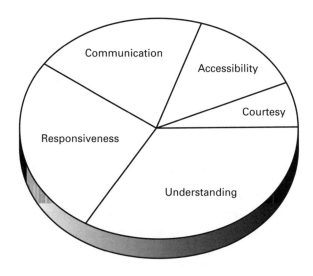

Customers understand that any product or service of value has associated costs. However, customer perspectives on price are frequently different from a bank's perspective. With respect to obtaining a home mortgage, this market defined price in terms of (a) interest rates (including points), and (b) fees (origination, surveys, inspections, appraisals, etc.).

In order to evaluate the bank's value position relative to three key competitors we employed the value matrix, combining customer perceptions of rate and fee fairness (relative to competition) on the vertical axis, and using a weighted average of benefit ratings on the horizontal axis. The result revealed a significant value disadvantage for the client bank (Figure 8-4).

Figure 8-4
VALUE POSITION: OVERALL

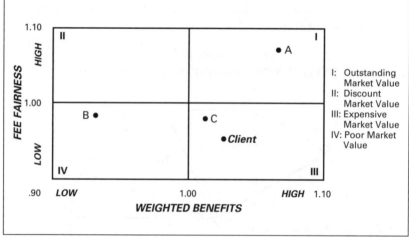

Bank A is the clear value leader in this product/market. This bank is perceived as providing a higher level of benefits at lower fees and interest rates (high level of fee fairness) than any competing bank. Bank B is perceived as providing poor market value, with low levels of perceived benefits at slightly higher than average fees and interest rates. Both bank C and the client bank are perceived as providing expensive market value. Within this value quadrant, the client bank is perceived as providing higher levels of benefits than bank C, but at higher fees and interest rates as well. This overall perspective indicates that the client bank must change the market's perception of fee fairness in order to move toward a position of outstanding market value, and it must also improve perceptions of benefits delivered if it is to overtake bank A's value position.

An overall perspective on value has limited use, however. Despite using *weighted* averages of market perceived benefits in the analysis above, this analysis doesn't provide *focus* on the most important benefits for subsequent evaluation of the value delivery system. Although value mapping is designed to identify opportunities to enhance benefits and reduce costs, it is desirable to focus attention on those components of value considered most important by the market and/or those on which the bank is competitively vulnerable. Consequently, separate analyses were conducted for *each* benefit dimension identified as important to this product/market. For the sake of explication, results for only the two most important benefit dimensions, understanding and responsiveness, are displayed in figures 8-5 and 8-6.

Figure 8-5
VALUE POSITION: UNDERSTANDING

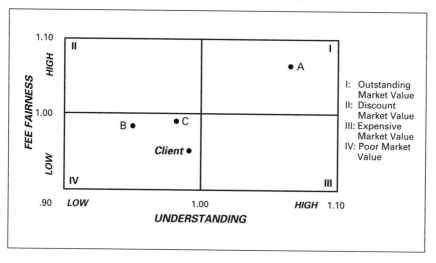

Figure 8-6
VALUE POSITION: RESPONSIVENESS

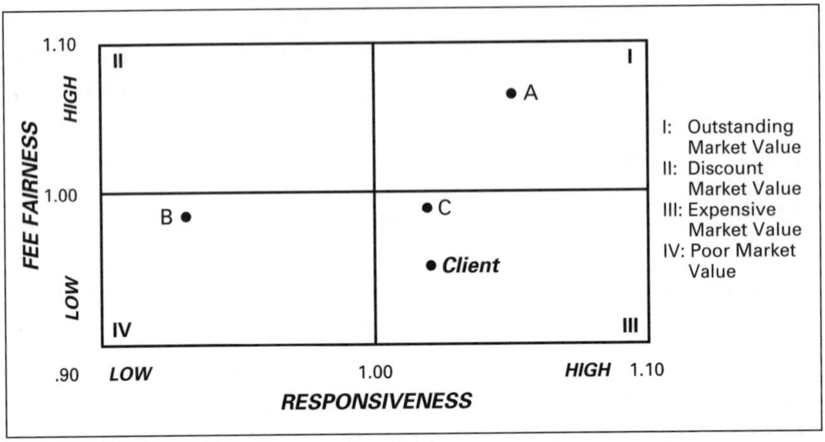

With regard to understanding, the most important determining dimension of value, the client bank is perceived as delivering poor market value. The levels of understanding displayed in the loan application process are perceived to be below average and the price of those benefits is substantially below the market average. With regard to responsiveness, the client bank is perceived to be providing expensive market value. The bank is responding slightly better than the market average, which is skewed slightly because of the relative unresponsiveness of bank B, but at or below the levels of responsiveness delivered by banks A and C.

These analyses suggest that, although value delivery could be improved on both benefit dimensions, the dimension of understanding required particular attention. Additional analysis based on the individual attributes of price revealed perceptions of unfairness relative to fees the client bank charged for loan processing services. The bank's interest rates were perceived to be about average relative to the competition. With this information in hand, the bank was prepared to evaluate its value delivery system, paying particular attention to opportunities for improving understanding and responsiveness while also identifying opportunities to reduce costs relating to fees charged.

The first step in *mapping* value delivery begins, again, with the customer. This step involves identifying key customer interfaces with the bank, sometimes referred to as "Moments of Truth." The process involves interviewing customers who have recently experienced the service delivery, preferably in focus groups, and charting their perceptions of contacts with representatives of the bank. An abbreviated map of key customer interfaces for this product/market is shown in Figure 8-7.

Figure 8-7
HOME MORTGAGE KEY CUSTOMER INTERFACES

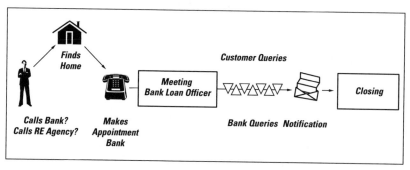

Note that the map includes all interfaces with the bank *from the customer's point of view* and progresses from initial contacts relative to mortgage origination through closing on the home purchase. Details have necessarily been omitted for purposes of clarity. For example, the meeting with the bank loan officer includes (1) ARM disclosure and application, (2) presentation of products, rates, and qualification (if not prequalified), (3) verification release forms, (4) government disclosure forms, (5) fees for credit check and appraisal, and (6) decision to lock or float interest rates. The triangles along the timeline between that bank meeting and closing represent variable additional contacts, whether originated by the bank for clarification of information (△) or by the customer inquiring about the loan status (▽).

Even at this stage of the analysis, two observations bearing on responsiveness, understanding, and price bear mention. First, there are very few customer contact points. Each contact is very important to customers because it provides an opportunity to demonstrate understanding of "unique" circumstances and to be proactively responsive to subsequent customer questions and concerns. Moreover, under circumstances of limited contact, the bank has fewer opportunities to correct mistakes or overcome bad impressions. Second, there exists a significant time lag between meeting with the bank's loan officer and receiving notification of loan disposition. During this period of time customers called the bank an average of four times to inquire about their loan status and received, on average, two calls requesting additional information. This is clearly a highly stressful time for the customer and the manner in which that time is handled can make or break a customer's perception of the bank.

. . . Includes Evaluation of Internal Processes . . .

The second step in value mapping is to identify all "back-room" activities relating to each customer interface. These include activities involving support personnel, information systems, reporting requirements, and a delineation of work flow. The purpose of this analysis is to identify all relevant steps in the value delivery process, and to assess the need for changes in the system leading to enhanced benefits to the customer or to reducing the costs to the bank of providing those benefits. An overview of the mapping process appears in Figure 8-8.

Development of the entire value delivery map requires extensive interviewing of bank personnel. Simply designing the map on the basis of the way "things are supposed to work" frequently obfuscates the reality of the workplace. Employees frequently develop shortcuts, information is thought to be captured that isn't, and different departments each assume that the other is monitoring the task. In the case of our client bank, for example, notice that there is no path representing systematic interaction with real estate agents or their firms. Real estate agents often serve as gate keepers. They can direct potential customers to "preferred" banks and discourage relationships with other banks. From the bank's point of view it is important to keep this gate open. In the absence of a value map, the bank's management *assumed* that loan officers maintained systematic contact with real estate agents, even to the point of including them in the initial meeting with the potential customer. In point of fact, however, loan officers often discouraged real estate agents from participating in the process because "they just get in the way." This was clearly a missed opportunity for demonstrating empathy and understanding by including, at no additional cost, a familiar face in proceedings that are often very confusing to the first-time home buyer. Addressing this oppor-

Figure 8-8
VALUE MAP

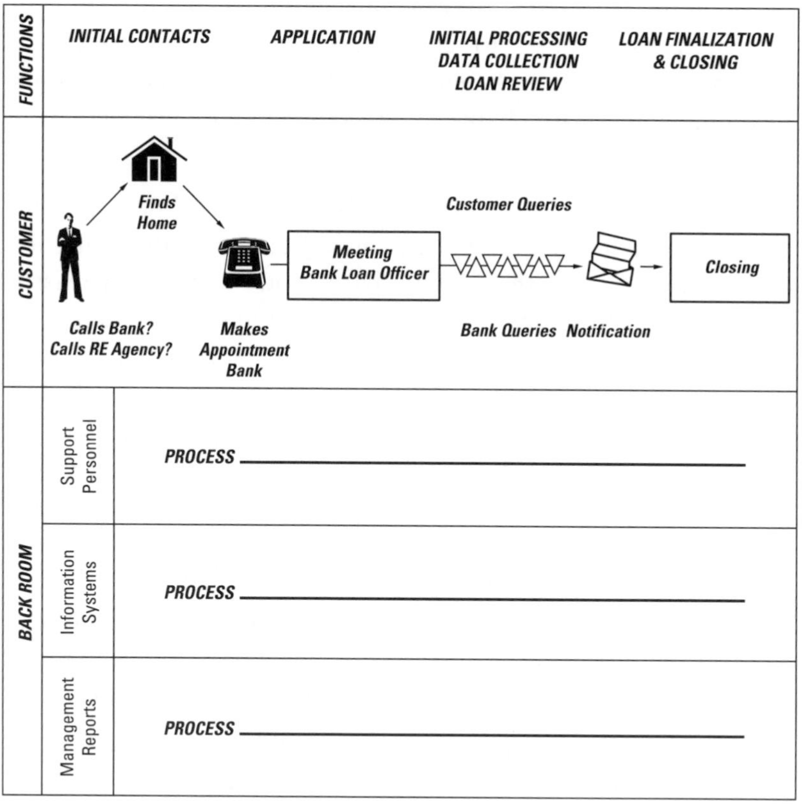

tunity can lead to increased customer referrals by making apostles of satisfied customers. In fact, the client bank later concluded that there existed a broader opportunity to network with local real estate firms, thereby bringing the entire loan application process into better alignment with market needs.

At the conclusion of internal interviews, all steps in the delivery process must be plotted on the map, including work and information flows. At this stage, the value map depicts the existing value delivery system, and can be evaluated in terms of efficiency and effectiveness. Evaluation of the value map should be conducted by an interfunctional team as part of the continuous improvement process described in Chapter 9. Objectives for the team are quite clear: identify opportunities to add value by enhancing the important benefits of understanding and responsiveness and/or by reducing the bank's cost of providing those benefits that, in turn, can be passed along to customers through fee reductions. Employees should also be encouraged to make observations and recommendations for changes that would enhance productivity or eliminate redundancies.

The client bank's value map consisted of 107 interconnected process components pertaining to mortgage origination and processing, with most of these being "back-room" activities. The issue of quality control is very important with this many steps. For example, even if at every step everything goes right 99 percent of the time, in a 107-step sequential process the odds are that only 34 percent of the time will the entire process perform correctly. This represents a significant amount of costly rework and potential customer annoyance. Also, the customer is unlikely to appreciate the complexity of this many steps when something does go wrong since most of these steps are invisible to him or her. This is not to suggest that the answer necessarily lies in the elimination of steps. If the process as a whole is to be effective, each step in the process must be executed correctly 100 percent of the time.

The bank's "Value Team" noted that several steps in the process were made necessary because procedures were not executed correctly the first time. These additional steps added unnecessary costs and, frequently, generated the appearance of being unresponsive to customers. One example of such a process step appears in Figure 8-9.

Figure 8-9
VALUE MAP: AN EXAMPLE OF A PROCESS STEP

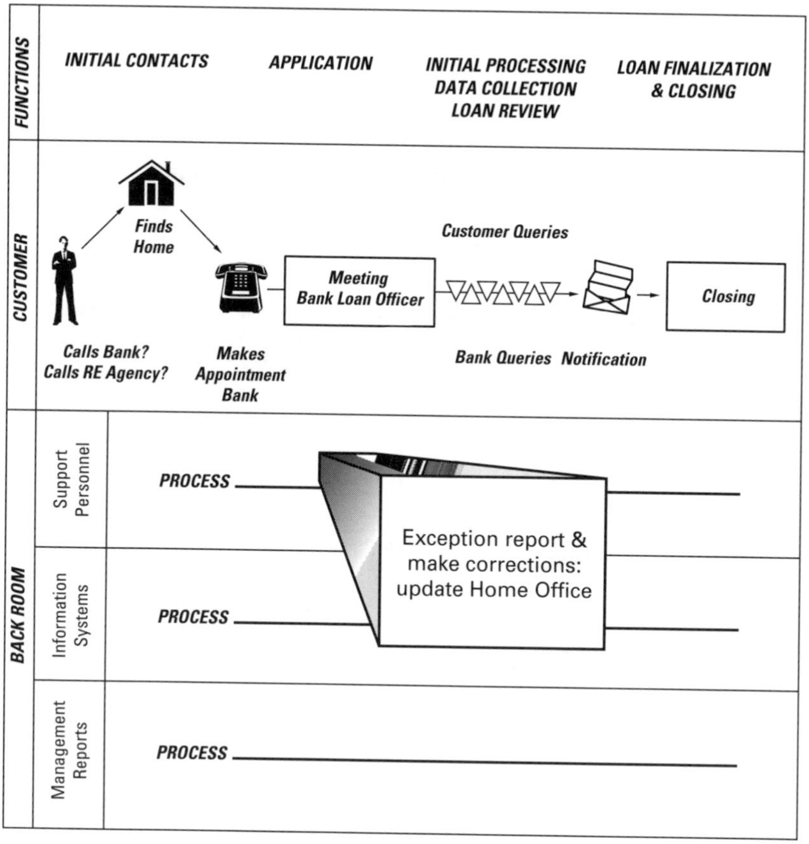

Exception reports issued by the compliance officer revealed a disproportionate number of undersigned loan applications and missing documentation. These exceptions led to additional steps designed to make the bank appear responsive. For example, loan forms were sent by Federal Express to minimize the turnaround time in getting appropriate signatures and the proper documentation, adding cost to the process that was translated into higher fees to the customer. Loan officers frequently had to spend time out of the office trying to track people down who, in turn, slowed down processing of the loan and frequently resulted in delaying appointments with other customers. These efforts to improve the appearance of responsiveness were actually resulting in being less responsive because of lost time, and in adding costs that translated into higher prices for the customer.

A second example from the Value Team's analysis demonstrates an opportunity for cost reductions through automation (Figure 8-10).

Figure 8-10
VALUE MAP: AN OPPORTUNITY FOR COST
REDUCTIONS THROUGH AUTOMATION

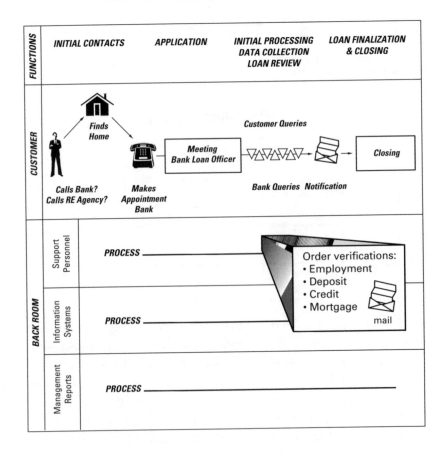

This step in the value map generated significant costs in personnel time as well as substantial mailing costs. Verification forms pertaining to employment, bank checking and savings accounts were generated, addresses confirmed, and letters sent seeking verification of information provided by the customer. Frequently, follow-up letters were required in order to generate a response. Since more than 80 percent of first-time mortgage buyers were employed locally, the bank's Value Team ascertained that much of this information could be generated electronically by establishing computerized links with major employers and banks in the local area. Not only would such electronic transfer of information reduce the costs of acquiring that information, but it would also speed the loan processing time, resulting in higher levels of responsiveness for the customer.

A third value-adding opportunity identified by the Value Team related to loan status reports (Figure 8-11).

The Value Map revealed that loan status reports were being generated biweekly and that these were reviewed by a loan processor to be sure that all steps were properly carried out. The loan processor retained this checklist in order to answer customer queries about the status of the loan. At no time, however, did the loan processor *initiate* a call to the customer to advise him or her of the loan's status. This was clearly a lost opportunity for demonstrating understanding of customer anxiety relative to the loan process, and to demonstrate a willingness to be responsive to customer questions and concerns. The Value Team proposed tracking customer inquiries for a two-month period to determine average elapsed time between customer-initiated calls and to implement a procedure of having the loan processor call the customer *just before* customers typically called the bank. The new procedure added value to the customer by demonstrating higher levels of understanding and responsiveness, both important benefit dimensions for this market.

Figure 8-11
VALUE MAP: LOAN STATUS REPORTS

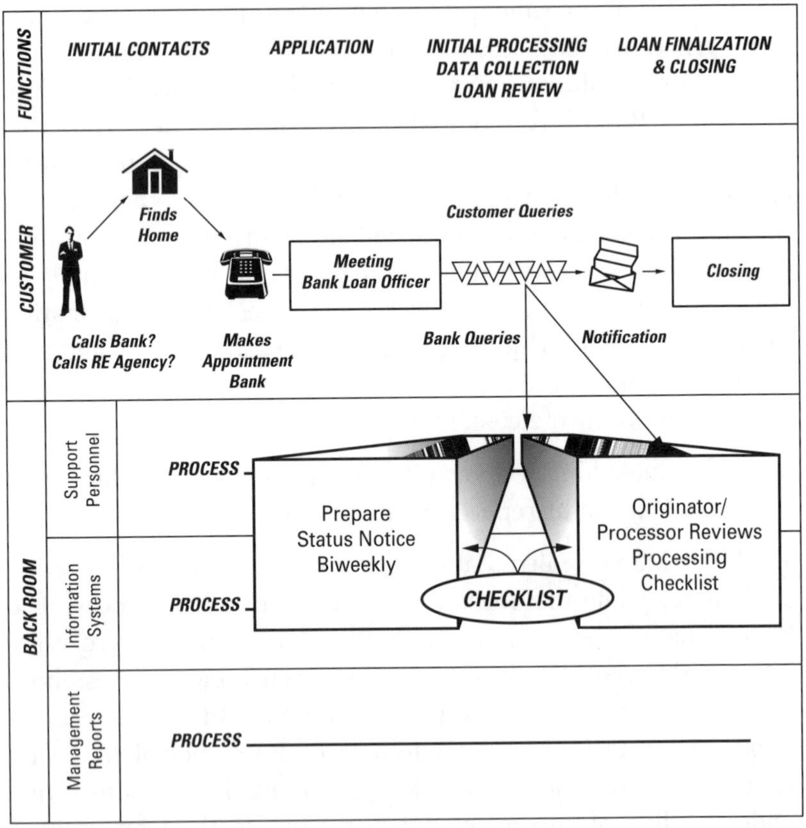

One final example from the client bank's value map demonstrates ineffective use of information (Figure 8-12).

For this example the emphasis is on the *flow* of information, and the example represents only one of several similar instances. The Value Team noted that the existing information systems were being used primarily to generate management reports. There was no evidence that information was being used to *drive* the business. For example, a computerized credit application log could be used to generate leads for real estate firms who have formed an alliance with the bank, thereby adding value to the real estate firm/bank relationship, resulting in more mortgage customers for the bank. More customers would result in economies of scale, thereby reducing fees for those customers. Similarly, loan rejections should be analyzed for patterns of disqualification that, in turn, should be systematically forwarded to the bank's loan officers. Such use of information would reduce costs associated with initial processing of questionable applications.

Figure 8-12
VALUE MAP: INFORMATION FLOWS

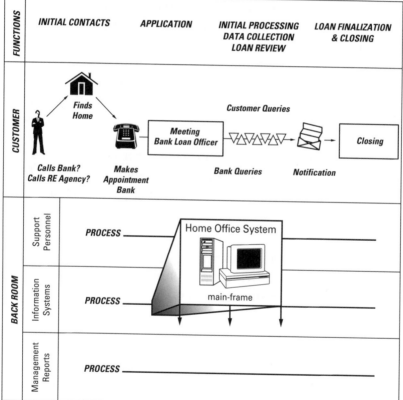

... And Ends with the Customer.

The detailed map of the value delivery system enabled the client bank to evaluate all delivery processes in terms of important dimensions of value. The bank's Value Team identified 16 specific steps in the value delivery process where unnecessary costs were incurred or where opportunities existed for enhancing important benefits to the customer. Analysis of these individual steps led to a redesign of the entire delivery system. Significant systemic changes in value delivery included (1) increasing the number of customer contact points from five to 10, (2) follow-up to the customer/loan officer meeting to answer questions and demonstrate understanding of unique needs, (3) utilization of new computer software to prompt proactive loan status reports, (4) systematically-including real estate agents in the value delivery path, (5) implementing new procedures for tracking lost leads, i.e., initial inquiries that did not materialize, (6) post-closing interviews and surveys to determine customer satisfaction with services rendered, and (7) redesign of information systems enabling easier access by all employees in the value chain. Additionally, the bank realized that there were too many process steps, with most being executed in the "back room," and a heavy reliance on outside suppliers of information. For example, employment verification required five steps and a significant time lag while waiting for responses from local employers. An automated verification process reduced the number of steps to two and the average verification time from two weeks to 1.5 days!

The Value Map also led bank management to the realization that value originates in *every employee*. For example, if the originating loan officer had understood the important dimensions of value for this product/market, he or she could have impacted both the costs associated with initial loan processing and the level of responsiveness provided by the bank. Similarly, the loan processor in charge of checking the status of loan applications thought that he or she was doing his or her job by merely having the information in hand in order to respond to customer inquiries. In the absence of information about the importance of demonstrating understanding and responsiveness, this loan processor failed to take the initiative to call customers with status updates. By making all employees aware of the important dimensions of value, each could focus on those that would provide the greatest value to the customer.

Finally, the process of value mapping to improve value delivery led the client bank to understand the importance of assessing its value position on an ongoing basis. After redesigning its value system, the bank again measured its value position from a market perspective, with the following result (Shown in Figure 8-13).

Figure 8-13
VALUE POSITION: OVERALL

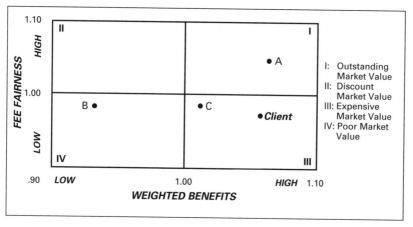

Two points regarding pre- and post-mapping measures are important. First, a comparison of Figure 8-13 (post-mapping value matrix) with Figure 8-4 (pre-mapping value matrix) shows that the client bank has improved its value position on both the benefits axis and the fee fairness axis. The client bank is perceived by the market as a better value now than it was before evaluating its value delivery system. However, the client bank is still perceived as being an expensive value provider. This brings us to the second point: It is always harder to move *toward* an outstanding value position than it is to start there. Changing market perceptions of value delivery is a difficult task that requires continuous effort over time. The client would have been well advised to evaluate market definitions of value *before* entering this product/market, tailoring its offering to important dimensions of value from the outset. It is always more expensive to overtake competition from behind than to start from an outstanding value position.

Summary

Value mapping is a process measure designed to improve value delivery by identifying opportunities to enhance benefits to the customer while reducing the price the customer pays for those benefits. The steps in designing and using a value map include:

- Identify key customer interfaces.
- Identify "back-room" activities related to the interface.
- Identify related information system requirements.
- Identify related management reporting systems.
- Determine the flow among system levels.
- Assess the need for change in the system.
- Implement the changes.

The development of value maps for each product/market helps to assure that you focus on important dimensions of value when evaluating your delivery system. Value mapping enables a cross-functional analysis of the entire delivery process, focusing employee attention on the customer's perspective of the process. Value mapping enables the identification and quantification of activity-based costs, and the identification of opportunities for improving the effectiveness of the delivery system. Finally, value mapping provides a blueprint for the development of strategic measures and controls of quality and cost.

9. CONTINUOUS VALUE IMPROVEMENT: THE ART & SCIENCE OF DOING WHAT MATTERS

> "Value is defined according to customers' needs rather than as a definite specification."
> -Anon

The "quality" revolution in America is rooted in the competitive threat posed by the Japanese in the early 1970's and continuing today. The Japanese philosophy has been well documented.[1] United States and Japanese companies operated with different views of quality.[2] The pervasive United States corporate view held "quality" as a static element. Given the static nature of quality expectations, quality standards could be specified and performance measures established for these established levels of desirable quality. The quality target was stable and identifiable, according to the United States corporate view, and once the standards were established it was simply a matter of attaining the desired quality standard.

The "quality" revolution in American companies was stimulated by a series of events that have their beginning in the early 1950s. Following World War II, United States companies were dominant in the world market and their financial performance reflected this dominance. Sales and profits were growing. As succinctly illustrated in the strategic value measurement chapter, United States companies were not using the correct instruments for measuring their success. The historically based financial measures made companies feel good and provided companies with a detailed map of the past. What was sorely missing in the United States Board Room was a map of the future.

United States companies failed to recognize the dynamic nature of customers' needs and expectations in establishing their static measures of "Quality Performance." The pervasive view of static quality levels held by United States companies throughout the 1950s and 1960s opened the door for competitive entry in multiple industries, including automobiles, electronics, microprocessors, and photocopiers. During this era, United States companies were financially successful in the short run, but these same companies were mortgaging their future by holding a static "satisficing" view of quality. The *value void* created during this period left the companies vulnerable for successful competitive intrusion by any firm willing to fill the void.

TENETS OF VALUE INTEGRATION

The literature is rife with the *cure du jour*. Many proponents of Total Quality Management have professed the wisdom of following a series of steps to achieve total quality in the organization.[3] For example, Joseph Juran—considered by many to be largely responsible for the quality movement in Japan—outlined the following steps for every CEO:[4]

1. Set up and serve on the company's quality council, the quality equivalent of the finance committee.

2. Establish corporate quality goals, including quality improvement goals, and make them a part of the business plan.

3. Make provisions for training the entire company hierarchy in managing for quality.

4. Establish a means to measure quality results against quality goals.

5. Review results against goals on a regular basis.

6. Give recognition for superior quality performance.

7. Revise the reward system to respond to the changes demanded by world-class quality.

Others have asked the question—"How do you get on the value train?" *The recommended answer is* to acquire a value discipline based on operational excellence, product leadership, or customer intimacy. Winners will be champions in one of these disciplines and competitive in the other two."[5]

The steps and lists are as numerous as the proponents of "quality" with Baldrige award winners[6] or insights gleaned from programmatic failures.[7] The plethora of solutions is confusing at best. Fortunately, the solutions offered are more similar than they first appear. The knowledge gained from our experience with the "quality" movement can be summarized in three fundamental tenets:

1. Customer Focus

2. Process Improvement

3. Deployment

The concept of value integration is grounded in the "living" of these three tenets and collocating a continuous improvement culture in the organization.

Customer Focus

Quality is a people issue. Everyone in the organization has either an internal or external customer. The value a customer derives from any consumption experience is inextricably linked to both a logical and emotional process. Organizational processes produce either a product or service for someone. Identify your customers, describe their needs and expectations, and define measures to assess the customer's degree of satisfaction. Harris Bank operates with a customer focus. The bank's guiding principles include the following statement: "The customer's voice drives all actions of the organization."[8]

As discussed throughout this book, a critical step for any bank to maintain a differential value advantage is the development of processes for identifying and communicating customers' needs and expectations. This seems like a simple thing, but remember simple does not mean easy. As illustrated in Chapters 5 and 6, customers have qualifying and determining dimensions with variability in the relative importance of their needs and expectations.

It is dangerous to assume that you "already know" which attributes or features of product/service, price, access, or information customers consider when making a purchase decision. Listening to the customer means opening channels of communication so that customers have direct input into the process of defining relevant attributes. This can be accomplished informally or formally (see Chapter 6). This process can prove invaluable in identifying all relevant *value dimensions* of customer expectations (see Chapter 5).

"Which customers should we ask?" is a question frequently raised. The answer is, "Customers representing your targeted product/market(s)"—whether or not they currently use your financial services. Although it is frequently easier to focus on your current customers, they may not adequately represent the product/market you wish to attract.

Banks with a value-oriented culture have a solid foundation for attaining sustainable differential value advantages (see Chapters 3 and 4). The culture of a value orientation provides a sharp and clear focus on the customer. Ultimately, the value-oriented bank's culture serves as a leverageable asset because it replaces counterproductive processes, releasing and focusing the creative power of each employee to find new and better ways to provide value to the customer and the organization.

Process Improvement

Organizations consist of hundreds of interrelated processes. Every process in the organization can be improved. *The question is not can you improve, but what should you improve from the customer's perspective.* For example, you could improve the process for issuing monthly statements to the point of providing delivery within 15 minutes after the close of business. Does this level of performance matter for my customers? At what price/cost?

Benchmarking is a technique for evaluating "best practice" on specific value attributes for the purpose of "stealing shamelessly" processes which lead to better value delivery. Although benchmarking has been around for some time, many companies using the technique fail to be systematic in the process. Benchmarking is a disciplined process requiring:

1. identification of important value-delivery attributes requiring improvement;

2. analysis of one's own practice and performance;

3. identification of "best practice" organization;

4. systematic site visits and interviews study *processes*, not *results*;

6. analysis of findings;

7. development of recommendations;

8. implementation; and

9. monitoring of results.

In evaluating processes you must recognize the difference between working on the process versus working on the outcome.[9] The distinction between measuring outcomes versus processes is very important for the organization. A good processes necessary, but does not guarantee a good outcome. Process performance evaluations have historically been based on identifying the flows, establishing performance criteria, applying statistical control techniques, and monitoring the results. The outcome measures are from the customer's perspective. Is the product or service reliable, on time, accurate, and at a reasonable customer price?

The name of the game is improvement, and the need is to reduce the time it takes to make improvements. Process benchmarking is a systematic approach to drive change into an organization. Identifying the "best process," making comparisons, and establishing performance output levels for the process are all critical for the effective application of benchmarking.

Figure 9-1
PROCESS VERSUS OUTCOME

Deployment

Train, empower, and reward your employees. This simple statement encompasses the key elements for effective deployment of one of the bank's most valuable assets—human resources. At Georgia-Pacific, employee teams can address *any issues that affect customers.*[10] Juran, in reviewing the differences between the Japanese and American response to the lectures and ideas proposed in 1954, pointed to key differences in the level of participation (CEO versus middle manager), the commitment to training, and the integration of quality into the review process.[11]

The concept of continuous improvement is predicated on the premise that people are more likely to change if they have a say in the change process. The true potential of continuous improvement is nested within cross-functional work teams, not just individuals. Cross-functional work teams, because of their influence on an organization and its members, are more effective primarily because of their inherent impact on the organizational climate.

Resistance, passive acceptance, and adoption of this shift in philosophy are to be expected in any organization. Some employees will be slow to accept the new ideas that might impact their existing work practices. However, experience has taught us that the distribution of employees on the basis of willingness to adopt typically follows the 70, 20, 10 rule. About 70 percent of those exposed to this new approach welcome it, 20 percent are undecided and take on a passive acceptance attitude, and 10 percent outright reject the new approach and will resist any attempts at change. With 70 percent of organizational employees willing and open to the new philosophy, the problem of creating cross-functional *value improvement teams* is not formidable.

It is relatively easy to start, but more difficult to maintain, the process of continuous improvement once initial interest abates. It is not a quick-fix customer awareness or "smile and dial" program. It is a continuous process that requires structure, commitment, and time. You are asking individuals to function as a team, change their way of thinking, and be committed to continuous change.

To empower employees generally requires alignment. Alignment refers to getting everyone oriented to one strategy or way of thinking. This could be a philosophy of management, a prevailing managerial style of leadership, or a program or process on how to deal with customer value. Do you treat employee training as an expense or as an investment?

The scarcest resource within any organization is productive people. Employee satisfaction leads to employee retention and higher levels of productivity which, in turn, leads to higher levels of customer value and lower costs. Although most bank managers are aware of the financial costs of employee turnover, few explicitly acknowledge the impact on productivity or on reduced levels of customer value. Fewer still make the effort to systematically evaluate employee satisfaction.

Employee satisfaction begins with recruitment which, in turn, should be driven by the bank's value infrastructure as discussed in Chapter 3. To the extent that there is misalignment between the value infrastructure and the bank's recruiting policies and practices, employees are certain to be dissatisfied and potential counterproductive. Kmart, for example, actively recruits college graduates into its management trainee program, ostensibly seeking highly motivated, bright, self-starting managers with initiative. Kmart's value infrastructure, however, demands uniformity and compliance with programs and practices initiated in Troy. This misalignment between the value infrastructure and employee recruiting practices inevitably has led to discontent among store managers.

The process of evaluating employee satisfaction is similar to the process of measuring customer satisfaction. As with value and customer satisfaction, the dimensions and attributes of work satisfaction must be defined by the employees. It simply won't do to have a group of managers decide what *should* be the dimensions of employee satisfaction and then query employees regarding their levels of satisfaction on those predefined dimensions. The dangers inherent in this approach are the same as those which apply to the measurement of customer satisfaction and value.

Following the identification of the dimensions and attributes of employee satisfaction, and the measurement of satisfaction levels on these attributes, you should examine the alignment of employee satisfaction dimensions with customer value dimensions. If customers value financial problem solving, but employees have not identified problem solving as a dimension which provides satisfaction, there is a lack of alignment between external and internal perspectives on value that is strategically unhealthy. If both groups have identified problem solving as an important dimension of satisfaction, but employees express dissatisfaction with their ability to solve problems, there may be other operational constraints that must be addressed.

Finally, measures of employee satisfaction must be balanced against measures of performance. Data pertaining to repurchasing behavior and overall satisfaction, for example, are used to provide evidence of the validity of the value dimensions. Similarly, management must decide upon specific external measures of employee performance against which the employee satisfaction dimensions can be validated. Obviously, these performance measures must be linked with important dimensions of customer value.

Absent effective deployment, the bank runs the risk of customer's experiencing apathy, curtness, impatience, incompetence, and unfriendliness. The majority of employees want to contribute to satisfying the customer and improving their work environment. Living the value message requires employee understanding and motivation.

The cost of nonchange (CONC), as described in Chapters 3 and 4, is the measurable cost to the bank of not satisfying customer (internal and external) needs and expectations (Table 9-1). Providing employees the opportunity through training, empowerment, and rewards, will result in the realignment of critical value processes and a dramatic reduction in overall cost.

Table 9-1
CONC (COST OF NONCHANGE)

Absenteeism	Customer Defection	Reconciliation
Employee Turnover	Explanation Time	Bank Liability
Complaint Handling	Grievances Lost	Unused Materials
Corrective Maintenance	Lost Sales	Waste
Customer Dissatisfaction	Nonproductive Time	Unplanned Overtime
	Queing	
	Workforce Pride	Unplanned Service

The recognition of the cost of nonchange facilitates the development of relevant questions with respect to the estimation of CONC. For example, what is the relationship between training and employee retention, and how is the consistency of customer service related to deposits or fee income? There is also a need to document critical customer paths, establishing value maps (see Chapter 8) that indicate which customer interfaces are most critical to customers' value perception and bank profits.

Kmart experiences excessive employee turnover at the associate level each year. The company accepts this as a cost of doing business with the rationalization that Kmart is a first-time employer. On closer examination, however, one can see the fallacy in accepting excessive employee turnover. The human resource can be a tremendous asset for the organization in the highly competitive arena for value differentiation. The turmoil of employee turnover translates to confusion and misalignment at the point of customer contact. Giving employees "happy buttons" in the absence of organizational commitment to continuous improvement will not change the outcome.

The ultimate effect of empowerment was summed up by Sarah Nolan, Amex Life Assurance when she stated, "It's a staggering thing how far people will go if they own the results."[12] You cannot simply tell employees that you are now a High Value Bank. You must be willing to live the message, provide the appropriate tools through training and empowerment, get involvement, and structure the reward system to encourage team building and performance. In short, align the critical systems and processes necessary to deliver outstanding customer value.

UPPING THE ANTE

To understand the role of "continuous improvement" in this revolution we will explore the evolution of the value paradigm in the United States. A simplified view of the evolution of the value philosophy is illustrated in Figure 9-2.

Self-Aggrandizing—Boy Are We Good!

In the 1950s and 1960s, Xerox was growing, with increasing sales and profits. The company had no measure of customer satisfaction. Xerox machines broke down regularly—company solution was a well-trained field service force to fix the machines. Customers would lease extra machines to avoid down time thus, Xerox obtained more profits. Key point missed by Xerox executives—Xerox's customers did not want repairs; they wanted machines that did not break down in the first place. The Japanese skirted the Xerox patents and developed machines that did not break. The results were devastating for Xerox.[13]

Figure 9-2
EVOLUTION OF THE VALUE PHILOSOPHY

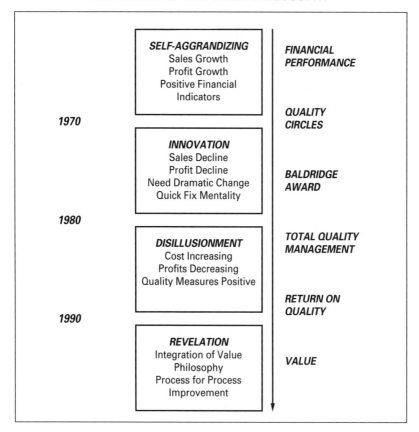

Xerox was not the only United States company that focused on financial measures of success and ignored the strategic implications of customer's changing needs, expectations, and definitions of value. The auto and electronics industries were equally confident that no competitor could match "Made in America." During the 1950s and 1960s profits were high and sales were growing. The old adage held true, it was what U.S. companies did not know that hurt them. As discussed previously, corporate America was missing a forward view and continued to steer using a map of the past (see Chapter 6). Japan's paradigm shift came as a surprise to American industry, though the Japanese and Americans attended the same series of lectures on quality and were privileged to the same support.

Innovation: Quick-Fix Mentality

Once United States companies started experiencing loss of market share and eroding profits, the answer seemed to be one of replicating the Japanese model. We talked the talk of quality and relegated the responsibility for quality to the "quality improvement group." This was the era of quality circles. The desire for innovative solutions was reflective of the American reliance on quick fixes. We were certain that quality could be achieved quickly.

Prestigious quality awards were established to help us measure our success. Winning the awards become a mission. In the scramble to "fix the problem" United States firms lost sight of the purpose and were caught up in the process.[14] Baldrige award winners, symbols of United States quality, were filing for bankruptcy protection. Something was wrong and disillusionment was the result.

Disillusionment

For many companies the push for quality was as badly misguided as it was well intended. Quality devotees grew obsessed with methodology—cost-cutting, defect reduction, quicker cycle times, and continual improvement. Before too long, customers' concerns seemed to fall by the wayside. Companies were investing tremendous resources into the evaluation of processes, identification of cause and effect, and improving processes throughout the organization only to find that if the "quality improvement" mattered little to customers the result was wasted effort and expense. "There's been an insufficient focus on the aspect of quality improvements that will make the largest contribution to overall financial performance," admits Curt W. Reimann, director of the Baldrige Quality Award.[15]

Banking giant NationsBank Corp. measures every improvement in service, from adding tellers to offering new mortgage products, in terms of added revenue. This new focus on Return on Quality (ROQ) is rooted in a financial measurement philosophy. The organization must ask—"How much is survival worth?" Do all competitors have the same constraints—technology, process, financial? What if a competitor makes the investment? How much of a return is enough? Customers are not concerned with your financial, process, and/or technological constraints. If you do not listen, the customer will find someone that will.

Revelation

The problem with listening to the customer: Sometimes you hear things you wish you had not. If differential value advantage means giving customers what they want, listening is a prerequisite. The focus on value has forced banks to rethink service. It might, for example, be something that occurs before the customer walks into the bank. A willingness to see the world from the customer's point of view and an eagerness to move swiftly are necessary attributes for successful value differentiation.

The bank and the customer both operate with a value function. The relationship between the organization's processes for adding value and the customer's perception of the value of the offering are illustrated in Figure 9-3. The *value cycle* highlights the relationship between the organization's value package and the customer's comprehension and willingness to buy. The organization's value package includes the initial product/service, the packaging, the channels of communication and the value added by intermediaries. The perceived value of this offering from the customer's perspective is not simply a set of numbers but includes the emotional aspects as well as competitive comparisons. If the customer perceives a fair value (minimally) for the offering an exchange will occur. Once the product/service is acquired the customer will gain experience during consumption. The experience with the product/service provides confirmatory or disconfirmatory evidence of the cognitive and emotive attributes utilized in the original purchase decision.

Figure 9-3
THE VALUE CYCLE

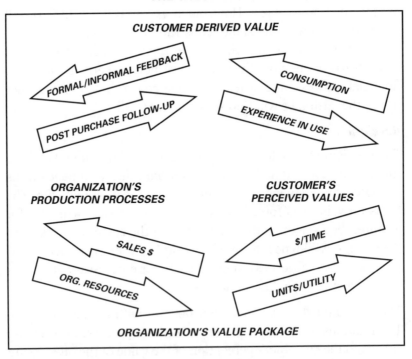

Maximizing customer satisfaction across the board could cost you a lot of money. The opportunities for differential value advantages can only be identified by listening to the customer. Post purchase follow-up, focus groups, surveys, and other formal and informal methods of listening to the customer are employed to identify the improvements that matter to the customer. "It's only value added if the customer perceives it as such," says Carlos Fallas, vice-president of sales for Con-Way Transportation Services.[16] You can never pursue quality to the exclusion of cost, or cost to the exclusion of quality. What we are after is improved value.

CONTINUOUS IMPROVEMENT PROCESS

The continuous improvement process is a vehicle for process improvement (Figure 9-4). The continuous improvement process relies on obtaining, communicating, and analyzing valid data. Many of the tools necessary for implementation of a continuous improvement process were discussed in Chapter 6. Basic tools such as flowcharts, checksheets, run charts, Pareto charts, histograms, scatter charts, cause/effect charts, control charts, factor analysis, cluster analysis, and other statistical procedures can be powerful. The process of continuous improvement involves the following steps:

- Identify processes.
- Identify process flows.
- Identify customers' needs and expectations.
- Link customers' needs and expectations with processes and identify key contact points.
- Establish process performance measures.
- Identify and evaluate value opportunities.
- Implement process modifications and monitor.

The identification of customer needs and expectations is a significant step in the continuous improvement process. Beyond identifying customers' needs and expectations, the bank must anticipate how changes in customer needs and expectations will affect the way they compete and win in the future. The anticipation of outcomes facilitates the formulation of proactive strategies for success. The organization, by carefully listening to the customer, has a better understanding of the derived and perceived value of their product/service (see Figure 9-3). Additionally, by anticipating the effects of changes in customers' needs and expectations the organization is able to leverage differential value advantages.

Figure 9-4
THE CONTINUOUS IMPROVEMENT PROCESS

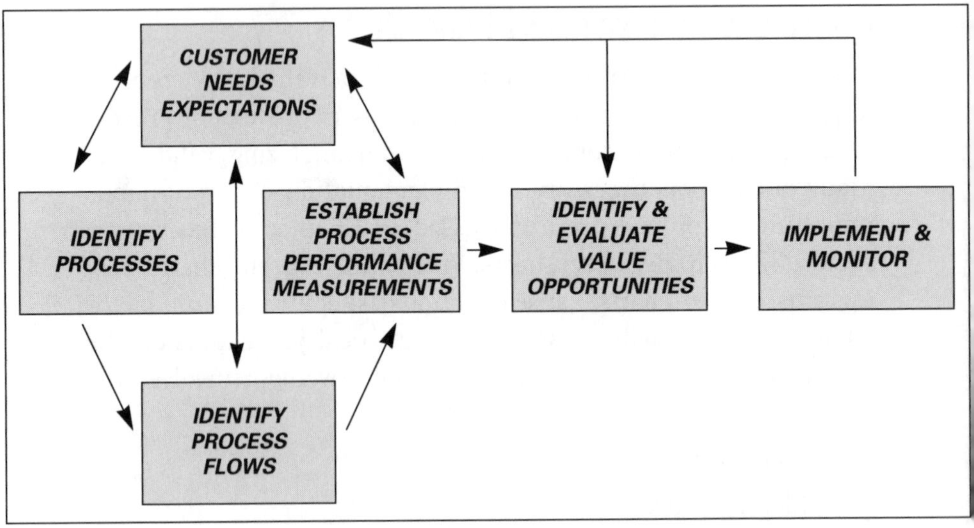

The "reactive organization" responds to environmental trends once the organization experiences negative financial results. The "learning organization" is postured to be proactive and adaptive in anticipation of environmental trends. The distinction between a "reactive" versus a "learning" organization is clear. The reactive organization will have difficulty in achieving a sustainable differential value advantage. Instead of skating to where the puck will be, they will always be chasing it. This attitude did not make Wayne Gretsky great and it will certainly not make your bank great! The very nature of following a pattern of reactive response is antithetical to the concept of competitive positioning for a sustainable differential value advantage. A reactive response typically attempts to create parity with competition as the first step. A position of "me-too" parity or "we're no worse than anybody else"

is not a differential advantage. Even the assumption that our competitors are all reactive, positioning the organization in a reactive mode, leads to strategic complacency.

The learning organization is proactive by anticipating the effect of environmental trends. Utilizing environmental information in a proactive posture is consistent with the concept of competitive positioning for a sustainable differential value advantage. A proactive strategy typically creates a differential value advantage relative to competition. The effective application of environmental intelligence in a learning organization results in placing the competition in a defensive, reactive posture. Predicting environmental trends coupled with the anticipation of likely outcomes is central to the culture of a learning organization. The learning organization benefits from the application of environmental intelligence for proactive strategic moves. A learning organization is driven by the corporate thesis: predict—anticipate—implement—grow.

SUMMARY

A willingness to see the world from the customer's point of view and an eagerness to move swiftly are necessary attributes for successful value differentiation. The "quality" movement can be summarized in three fundamental tenets:

1. Customer Focus: *Everyone in the organization has a customer.*

2. Process Improvement: *Doing what matters for our targeted customers.*

3. Deployment: *Train, empower, and reward your employees.*

The concept of value integration is grounded in the "living" of these three tenets and collocating a continuous improvement culture in the organization.

The *value cycle* highlights the relationship between the organization's value package and the customer's comprehension and willingness to buy. The learning organization will be proactive in the recognition of value voids and leverage these value opportunities for differential advantage. The continuous improvement process is the enabling process to attain and sustain differential value advantage.

Organization's and customers' needs and expectations change. You can always strive to improve the perceived and derived value of your offering. Changing to be changing does not equate with differential value advantage. Process improvements add value when the customer perceives the improvement as pertinent and consequential.

Endnotes

1. Imai, M. (1986) *KAIZEN: The Key to Japan's Competitive Success*, Random House.

2. Juran, Joseph M. (1993) "Made in the U.S.A.: A Renaissance in Quality," *Harvard Business Review* (July/August).

3. Tenner, Arthur R. and Detoro, Irving J. (1992) *Total Quality Management*, Addison-Wesley Publishing Company.

4. Juran, Joseph M. (1993) "Made in the U.S.A.: A Renaissance in Quality," *Harvard Business Review* (July/August).

5. Jacob, Rahul (1993) "Beyond Quality & Value," *Fortune* (Autumn/Winter).

6. Hodgetts, Richard M. (1994) Quality Lessons from America's Baldrige Winners, *Business Horizons* (July/August).

7. Beer, Michael; Eisenstat, Russell A. and Spector, Bert (1990) "Why Change Programs Don't Produce Change," *Harvard Business Review* (November–December).

8. Hinton, Tom and Schaeffer, Wini (1994) *Customer-Focused Quality*, Prentice Hall, Inc.

9. Geraves, David (1993) "Forget the Myths and Get on with TQM-Fast," *National Productivity Review* (Summer).

10. Angelillo, Donna-Marie and Mapes, Rick (1993) "Georgia-Pacific Uses Teamwork for Continuous Improvement," *National Productivity Review* (Autumn).

11. Juran, Joseph M. (1993) "Made in the U.S.A.: A Renaissance in Quality," *Harvard Business Review* (July/August).

12. Rose, Frank (1991) "Now Quality Means Service Too," *Fortune* (April).

13. Juran, Joseph M. (1993) "Made in the U.S.A.: A Renaissance in Quality," *Harvard Business Review* (July/August).

14. Greising, David (1994) "Quality: How to Make it Pay," *Business Week* (August 8).

15. *Ibid.*

16. (1993) "Value Added: A Powerful Pitch or Just More Puff?," *Purchasing* (February 18).

10. CHANGE: AT YOUR OWN RISK

> "You can't change current problems with current thinking because current problems are a result of current thinking."
> -Einstein
> "Never try to teach a pig to sing. It wastes your time and annoys the pig."
> -Anon

The twenty-first century will begin with a continuation of the turmoil and challenge that had its roots in the 1960s. The Age of Social Transformation will continue. Challenges looming ahead could well be more exciting and challenging than those already experienced.

Everyone has a tendency to talk themselves out of change. A day-to-day narrow focus gives a close-up view of an organization and the business it conducts. As the lens is widened it is easier to see the landscape in a continually broader context of the systems, processes, and purpose in which it operates. This is the process view of change that is necessary in order to be successful into the twenty-first century. Admitting to change is paramount to admitting to past wrongs. Experiencing change, doing things differently, participation in unaccustomed activity, and being on unfamiliar ground is often both exciting and frightening because it is perceived as risky. Transformations always are.[1]

We have lived both inside corporations and as consultants for nearly a combined century. Deregulation in telecommunications and banking, invasion of the Japanese into the rust-belt, the retailing revolution, and the concerns with ethics, diversity, multi-culturalism, and social justice are a few of the issues we have addressed in the corporation and in the classroom. This chapter is an act of synthesis; it sorts through experiences that have, and have not, worked to put together a concise definition of what change means.

First there must exist an understanding within the organization of its orientation and traditional paradigms. Many assumptions relative to philosophy and orientation are taken for granted and never articulated until there is an effort to do so. Orientation is the *what* presented in Chapter 1, and the *why* and *how* are addressed in this chapter. Second, it's not enough to want change, to be dis-contented with present conditions. We strongly believe there has to be a path, a way for change to succeed. Existing paradigms serve as blinders in every organization. Blinders can be the significant difference between an intellectual paradigm and a practicable paradigm, between what we say and what we really do, between rhetoric and reality. Unlearning old habits and paradigms is no easy task, and this chapter discusses issues for consideration in changing the twenty-first century organization.

PHILOSOPHY

Philosophic orientation can assume any of several profiles, predominately production, sales, and market as discussed in Chapter 1. The organization can also have attributes that lean the organization toward technology, regulation, or systems orienta-tions. Each organization has its own unique attributes, culture, and history. These elements, when combined, form the orientation and philosophy driving responses to different issues, with different requirements, and producing varying results. Every organization, like every person, has some degree of myopia that limits the success of that organization or person.

Orientation is the place to begin in assessing the organization's willingness to change. It is an important perspective because it is the foundation for further analysis and definition of the business. It is a significant indicator of the type of culture housed within organizational walls, and the types of barriers the corporation faces in a fiercely competitive global environment. Each orientation, with its unique attributes, has additional characteristics that must be assessed in order to realistically apprise what types of changes, if any, are needed, and how to make those changes.

While orientation is indicative of *willingness* to change, organizational personality is indicative of *ability* to change. Analogous to a human personality, the profiles of an organization are not unidimensional. They are multifaceted. Rather akin to the mythological Hydra, the monster of many heads that was slain by Hercules, multifariousness can be a difficult monster to deal with. The versatility of the human personality is both positive in that it allows considerable adaptation, and negative in that it can be as limiting as it is limitless. Organizations display this same versatility.

Defenses are present in all humans and organizations, and these defenses are considered a necessary part of survival. A defense is pathological only when: (1) there is no awareness of the defense, combined with and (2) the belief that it does not exist. Use of these defenses varies, however, the issue being the level of awareness associated with the defenses and how that awareness is used in coping with day-to-day issues of existence and survival. Internal awareness also determines the capability of the organization to achieve ever greater levels of maturity. For example, avoidance is a defense when it is used in a temporal fashion to deal with a perceived threat. It is a disorder when the avoidant is unable to perceive and deal with issues in such a way that an issue is understood and accepted without undue anxiety in a reasonable time period. Avoidance is manifested by saying and believing one thing, but underneath there is another pattern that more often than not is denied. It takes courage to see the reality that denial.

Disorders are severe or extreme forms of defenses. Severity can be to the extent that the organization has a very limited ability to cope, or beyond to the extent that it has no ability to cope with reality.[2] Tentacles of disorders and defenses are subtle, layered, and penetrating. Disorders are places of great struggle and tension and friction. There are a number of more or less adaptive ways to deal with the organizational friction, and they are discussed below.

Organizations with cultural disorders have little or no ability to see reality. Banks with a sales or production philosophy will likely be blind to value opportunities. This inability is often not apparent, especially when the vocabulary seems to be in place. Vocabulary can make assessment more difficult, but an ersatz New Age approach can be determined by whether listening skills are present, whether the actions overshadow the words, and by looking at the direction rather than at the steps.[3]

Balance

A healthy organization depends on the balance between internal perspectives and the external world. When there is a mutual understanding of reality between the two, the organization is in balance. In a balanced organization the partners ask what they can bring to the partnership as well as what can they obtain. Balance implies certain leadership qualities, but it is the rare leader who is willing to redefine reality, to tackle the arduous and complex task of reexamination. There is a struggle to gain, or to avoid, ever greater levels of maturity, with often lengthy periods of confusion and frustration. There are no single easy answers in the struggle to define and give direction to an organization.

One example of a company and a CEO that is apparently willing to do just such a self-examination is Emerson Electric and Chuck Knight. Traditionally, Emerson had financially oriented, best cost reviews. Within the past few years, Knight realized that future growth must now come from innovation. Reviews were revamped to reflect a balanced perspective of cost and innovation. Emerson had been a very successful company with the best cost approach, and only through a painstaking reexamination could such a shift in emphasis occur.

New Age management ideas are often gossamer concepts imposed by people who have never had a front-line job. First, they create a mythical world that contains ideal organizations where there is no confrontation, no aggression, everyone is empowered to do as they please, decisions are optimal only under Theory Y, everyone is cooperative, and sees the vision and mission with commonality, and only win-win situations exist.

These ideas have taken on a life of their own in the literature and often in the classroom, with an especially appealing sales pitch.

FLASH! BULLETIN! Conflict is inevitable in every relationship. All individuals and organizations are both masters and servants of power. Competition is definitely present within organizations and is manifested in the allocation of resources, especially time and money. We are all human and must expect and accept criticism. Search for the often hidden Stargate to reality is an aggressive process that causes disturbances. It is judicious, rather than unequivocal giving, withholding, praising, and criticizing. We hope that these well-packaged but nonsubstantive New Age-type ideas wind up like all endangered species—on a stamp.

This is not a shot at companies with a social conscience such as Ben & Jerry's, Tom's of Maine, or Levi Strauss. Such companies have great visions and we applaud their efforts. What we are saying is that change means confrontation, challenge, and sometimes even being offended. Our experience is that seldom do people begin with the intent to offend others, and when people are offended we encourage them to consider intent. Listening, trying to understand the message and the intent, and then trying to be understood make confrontation and challenge worthwhile. It is important to recognize that not everybody is the same. There are different expectations and biases that once understood, if not agreed upon, tend to have diminished importance. The concepts perpetrated must have a sense of reality rather than reliance on utopian implementations.

Unlearning

Learning is a fundamental ability of humans that, within the right organization, synergizes in a logarithmic fashion. Learning as an organization is addressed in the chapter on continuous improvement, but the issue that needs to be raised here is the ability to unlearn.

Each person within an organization makes millions of assumptions conditioned by experiences. Experience leads to habits and thinking patterns that anchor the limits of the individual. And it is important to remember that the experiences used as the bases for decisions are not necessarily a result of working in the current organization. Experience and learned assumptions are carried forward from other times and settings. Unlearning is a critical issue for individuals because change implies that what we know from the past will no longer apply to the same degree in the future. Qualifying for future success depends on unlearning, on not allowing objects in the rear-view mirror to appear closer than they are.

An example of a leader who displays the ability to unlearn is Don Shula, coach of the Miami Dolphin's football team. As the coach with the most lifetime wins, Shula has had to learn, unlearn, and relearn many times during his long career. Most managers do not possess the same ability to adapt to changing conditions over the decades of their career. The ability to unlearn is a necessary on ramp to the path of consistent and long-term success.

The principal basis for unlearning is awareness through listening. Most of us listen poorly because we are lazy and listening is hard work, and because people don't realize they aren't listening. Listening, however, is only half of the equation. Communicating is invariably a two-way street, a reciprocal phenomenon that requires understanding and being understood. Many managers are unwilling or unable to expend the energy required to listen to others, and usually listen selectively with a preset agenda in mind.

Unlearning incorporates commitment and that means making the vision your number one work priority. It means devoting time and energy. If you intend to stay in your organization, you have to be willing to persevere. Ups and downs of change can be very steep and risky. A person reaching too high can fall a long way, as did the mythological Icarus when he reached for the sun. Conversely, fear keeps ideas in a drawer, and keeps people from full-fledged commitments. Fear seems to precipitate people feeling if they make one mistake they could be sprouting wings and playing a harp.

In the quest for a fix, we have seen top managers bring in consultants to introduce a new system, such as total quality management (TQM), thinking that the system itself will change the results without the managers themselves having to change at all. A process or a system alone will certainly not change the culture of an organization. Harmonious orchestration in the way front-line work is being done, coupled with the attitudes and modeling of top management is what gets results. "The only thing that really works in bringing about significant, long-lasting change is a working environment in which people can integrate their work and their lives in ways that provide meaning and fulfillment and dignity and worth."[4] We couldn't agree more.

And the specifics of what works with one organization may not work with another. In a recent meeting with a Fortune 50 company, the CEO spoke on his vision and every vice president that spoke made statements antithetical to that vision. None of them could even see the inconsistencies. That alone is enough to doom any process, system, or rhetoric that is supposed to instigate change.

ORGANIZATION

There is a circulating myth that there is a "normal" organization, but the myth is only true if normal means balanced. Every organization has a unique set of values, different stories, and different ways of looking at the world. No matter how insignificant they may seem, these stories, woven together, are a powerful part of the fabric we call the culture of a company. This culture is the community in which the company's work is done. To be committed to the vision means actively seeking to understand the organizational story, and this is true whether it's a Fortune 50 company or a hometown bank. And upon assessing several hundred companies we honestly believe there are few truly balanced organizations. Organizations seem to have a knack of getting trapped in webs of their own creation, living in the concept rather than in reality.

An organization is a group of unique partners who have made a commitment to maintain the relationship. Many organizational families rely on denial of problems as a survival mechanism. Denial is a way of coping with secrecy. Denial of one secret leads to denial in other areas, thus stifling honest communication and ultimately learning to deny their own reality. It is common for established paradigms in the organization to repeat themselves in the next generation, and the organization becomes blind to the process. Increasingly sophisticated techniques of denial are learned. And yet if that same amount of energy were devoted to listening, assessing and internalizing, the results would be infinitely better.

Paradigm Construction

In personal psychology it is popular to call paradigms maps. We outline in this section some guidelines for mapmaking, with emphasis that they are *guidelines* rather than *rules*. Again, what works very well for one organization might not be as successful for another, but the guidelines are the result of patterns we have seen and experienced in many companies.

There is a need for a new paradigm in a new time with new realities. The modern era of social transformation and globalization has created circumstances whereby survival is dependent upon the ability to construct and use revised paradigms. Indeed in times gone by it might well have been enough to open alternatives, but now more than ever it is necessary not only to open alternatives but to make creative and coherent choices among those alternatives. In an otherwise balanced organization, choice confusion is the result of a flawed or outdated paradigm. Beginning the task of updating is rather like walking into a dark room where your eyes must gradually adjust. As adjustments are made and the paradigm changes, behavior and actions will also change.[5] Neither buzz-words nor smile training will produce desired changes in behavior, but will keep you in the illusion that no further change is needed. As Scott Peck says in *The Road Less Traveled*, "Our view of reality is like a map with which to negotiate the terrain of life. If the map is true and accurate, we will generally know where we are, and if we have decided where we want to go, we will know generally how to get there."

Making and remaking maps requires effort—often extraordinary effort. The more effort we make to appreciate and perceive reality, the larger and more accurate our maps will be. But most do not want to make this effort, or simply cannot make the effort because they do not understand the consequences of not doing so.

Truth or reality is often avoided when it conflicts with what is desired. Most managers will perceive problems with their organization for months or years before they take any effective action, if they ever do. We can revise our maps only when we have the discipline to overcome our natural defenses. To have such discipline, we must be totally dedicated to the truth. Organizational health is an ongoing process of dedication to truth and reality at all costs. All of us attempt to avoid problems to one degree or another. This tendency to avoid problems and the suffering inherent to that avoidance is a primary basis of most organizational demise.

Change requires a critical mass to be self-sustaining. It is a chain reaction similar to diffusion of an innovation. Generally, between 5 and 20 percent of a population is needed for critical mass. The time from critical mass to 80 percent is variable, but our experience is that large organizations take five to seven years to instill and live a change of paradigm. Attitude affects choices, and top management's attitude and modeling are half the impetus to change. The other half is the front-line worker who very likely knows the changes that are required within the front line environment. Sandwiched between those two is the proverbial middle management. These managers, like teachers in the general population, are protectors, perpetrators, and disseminators of status quo. This is obviously not true for every middle manager, but in general it is the posture middle management takes toward change. They believe they have vested interests and they go to great lengths to protect those interests. They are, however, careful observers of top management patterns and choices because one day they too aspire to join that elite group. Programs initiated by middle management are often subtly complex in their propagation of the status quo, and are based on a combination of fact, fear, perceived marching orders, risk, and intuition. Misperceptions and intuition are the subtle factors most responsible for inhibition of change. Remember, intuition is based on the maps we employ, and if the maps are distorted with defenses or disorders intuition leads in the wrong direction. With sensation we see corners, but with intuition we see around corners. With sensation we can read the lines, with intuition we can read between the lines. We must ask whether the efforts toward change are really just doing more of the same, or are we reading between the lines?

Managers who have conflicting attitudes or values or display contradictory behaviors that compete for their employees allegiance are precipitating avoidance. All unhealthy families have in common their inability to discuss root problems, and the same is true for larger organizations. It is the shroud of secrecy that gives rise to the inability to talk about the problems. A dysfunctional organization has severely restricted and systematically distorted communications. We easily but erroneously assume that if it isn't working and we aren't happy, somehow we haven't done enough yet. We become unable to discern when someone or something is good or not good for us.

Some academics, again it seems to be those lacking front line experience, advise us to stop managing and controlling. But often their context seems to end up meaning not helping and not giving advice. If as teachers we believed this we would certainly be ineffective. The role of the teacher, almost by definition, involves social influence. A teacher's job is to influence students. Judicious use of power is an inherent part of the teaching process. Let me rephrase that. The role of the manager, almost by definition, involves social influence. A manager's job is to influence employees. The statement "If you give a man a fish he will eat today, but if you teach him to fish, he'll eat for the rest of his life" has powerful implications. Judicious use of power is an inherent part of the managerial process. Theory X is out and Theory Y is the answer is only in the mind of the ivory towered academics. Beliefs and assumptions aren't what's important. It is the ability to question them that's important. Without consistent vigilance, resumption of old ways of thinking, feeling, and relating can be a nemesis. Just such a nemesis was present in the telecommunications divestiture. AT&T and GTE had very high turnover rates in the post-divestiture era because the old ways of thinking that were dominated by a regulation orientation were not easily reformed to do business in the newly competitive environment.

Discipline

Life is a series of problems we can either whine about or solve to the best of our ability. And it is in this very process of meeting and solving problems that gives life its meaning and makes living worthwhile. Think how boring the alternative of never having to solve a problem would be! Addressing and solving problems calls forth courage and wisdom that challenges and encourages our capacity. It is through confronting and resolving problems that we learn. When an individual learns the organization that individual is part of also learns. This is the essence of a learning organization.

But we all attempt to avoid problems to some degree. In fact, organizations seem to go to extraordinary lengths to avoid problems, building the most elaborate fantasies in which to live, sometimes to the total exclusion of reality. Avoiding the problems that growth demands is antithetical to the mission of most organizations. There is a need to face problems directly and in such a way as to work through them and solve them successfully, learning and growing in the process. Responsibility for the problem must be accepted before we can solve it. It can't be solved by saying it's not my problem. Almost a universal falsehood is that problems we face are caused by other people, by social circumstances beyond control, and therefore it is up to others to solve the problems so we can in turn blame them when the results are not to our satisfaction. Listening is usually the key ingredient in revising such an attitude and, combined with the guidelines below, can transform such an attitude to a productive state. Said another way, when the sale is made, the commitment only just begins. When vision is articulated, the path begins to come into view.

To foster the creativity and innovation required to change a paradigm, an organization needs to develop a "mistake center." In the mind's eye it's a huge glass and steel building with awesome reflections and a towering presence. But it requires no real estate or bricks and mortar. It only needs to exist in the mind's eye, a place where intelligent questioning, awareness, and learning are paramount activities. Without such a center there is no safe harbor for mistakes, and hence employees will take very few chances in stepping out in the direction of the vision. As Machiavelli so aptly stated nearly 500 years ago, "It must be considered that there is nothing more difficult to carry out, nor more doubtful of success, nor dangerous to handle, than to initiate a new order of things."

Guidelines Rather Than Rules

To attempt change we must first understand the complex components of our current system of thinking and then learn to modify the content and arrangement of those components. A big challenge! Our intent is for both the organization and the people within the organization to have the tools to make adjustments based on the perspective presented here. Managers are both a reflection of and a reflection on the organization. Some perennial advice to students has always been to match their personality to the personality of the organization if they desire harmony and satisfaction from their career.

Can you listen? The answer to this question might seem banally self-evident, but if so why do most major corporations spend oodles of money on training to enhance employees' listening skills? We believe every organization has the capability to change, but not all have the capacity. Capability is potential, capacity is ability in the present.

Are there any symptoms? Consider if there is dissatisfaction, blame, cover-ups, little job satisfaction, or a consistent pattern of criticism, e.g., in the press. There is a gap between a static organization and a changing world. That gap is evident in the recent histories of firms such as IBM, Sears, and American Express. These companies did not make a conscious decision to be static, they were simply oblivious to the signals that they might have heard. Maybe CEOs need the additional subtitle of EVP of change that is evaluated on a complacency scale. Intelligent questioning is seldom present in static organizations. To challenge cherished notions and assumptions, middle management change police must be shackled.

The process of organizational change is often difficult to describe in a generalizable manner. Depending on the source, change is usually described as some type of gradual, Darwinian evolution. The next author, looking for a hook, points out that the dinosaurs were undergoing gradual change when environmental circumstances made them extinct. Our belief is that change is a modified step function, with gradual change and improvement until environmental circumstances dictate a more revolutionary modification. Chase Manhattan Corp. appears to currently be in the throes of a revolutionary change. A bank with a proud heritage, Chase found the 1980s to be an unfriendly decade, culminating in nearly a billion dollars in loss in 1989–1990. With a new CEO in place in 1991, it embarked on the formidable task of defining its vision and values. The vision was established as becoming the best financial services provider in the world, based on the five values of customer focus, respect for each other, teamwork, quality, and professionalism. A monumental change such as the one experienced by Chase requires:

1. **Patience**—Profits at Chase are improving but the final verdict won't be in for three or four more years.

2. **Presenting a balanced picture of pro and cons**— Chase used an outside consultant to cut through the vested interest of a long-established heritage.

3. **Clearly communicating priorities**—Established vision and values that are communicated at every opportunity to every employee combined with performance for pay standards that support those priorities.

4. **Stating differences and allowing others to do the same**—An all important executive retreat to reinforce this is encouraged in training sessions and water cooler discussions throughout the organization.

Questioning is particularly important because it filters power into the hands of the people with valid assumptions of reality and prevents ossification of management attitudes.

As evidenced by the Chase example and many iterations with clients in similar circumstances, the progression of change follows the common sense shown in the following three steps:

1. **Where are we now?** Define orientation, vision, and values. A resultant definition of the culture will enlighten management by delimiting the primary defenses. This causes consternation initially, but eventually is worth every bit of the risk and frustration.

2. **Where do we want to go?** Reorientation based on the reality bounded in step 1, with a revision or specification of the vision and values. This is the place to define the mission and the corporate level opportunities. It involves a lot of collaboration and listening

3. **How do we get there?** Integration of the results of steps 1 and 2. Incorporate feedback from front-line employees and instill the processes and systems that support steps 1 and 2. This transformation requires continually checking in to validate the new paradigm.

While proceeding through phases of change there is overlap. Tom Peters[6] calls this chaos, and an organization may well retreat to earlier positions. That retreat can be frustrating, and it must be kept in mind that *moving from one development stage to another requires:*

1. **Time**—Five years is a reliable average.

2. **More than one setting**—Implementing in one branch, or store or plant is a beginning step, but the change process needs attention in several settings to attain the critical mass necessary to sustain the effort.

3. **Old paradigm must be available**—An oft repeated mistake is to expect front-line workers to accept whole-heartedly a new way of thinking and behaving. It doesn't happen that way and a great deal of unrest, rebellion, and even sabotage will occur unless the perceived risk is minimized. For example, changing a compensation plan to one that supports a new vision needs to be initially on a voluntary basis. When employees learn they will be rewarded for supporting the vision, most will willingly switch to the supportive system, especially with appropriate modeling behavior from superiors.

4. **Time to rest**—Progress won't be made every day on every front. Allow people and the organization time to assimilate the changes, but don't stonewall them.

5. **Permission to make mistakes**—Again, a mistake center is necessary. Remember, it's a new and changing world. Intelligent failure, i.e., thinking through a problem, defining alternatives, and choosing to behave consistently with the new paradigm, is acceptable and necessary.

6. **Opportunity to ask questions and get additional information**—If communication is restricted, any progress is incremental and change will not occur in a sufficient degree to realize the vision. This is an extremely uncomfortable aspect for many cultures that are historically expectant of rank and file obedience.

7. **Someone to provide limits and structure**—Beginning with the executive suite and filtering to every manager is the ability to discern sincerity from stonewalling. Too much control is deadly and too little is anarchy. Transformational leaders are rare and need to be identified early in the process.

8. **Celebration of success**—Again, money is important, but showing and telling people they have accomplished progress toward the vision is absolutely necessary. Sharing the success is imperative.

SOME CLOSING THOUGHTS

Costs of nonchange (CONC), which are explained in the chapter on value measurement, are often very apparent but unrecognized as substantial. Traditional return on investment (ROI) calculations give no recognition for improved throughput, increased value, or increased flexibility in terms of ability to respond to the market.

A culture of change, flexibility, and improvement are included in the vision of many organizations. There are no quick fixes to produce those attributes. The law of the farm harvest applies, sow before you can reap.

Loss awakens an organization by communicating an important message. There are probably more Chapter 7 and 11 filings resulting from these nondynamic paradigms than from any other circumstances. A quick gain should also communicate because it often contains the same message. Mulishly resisting such messages besieges the organization with wrong analysis, bungled interpretations, and false conclusions. If we wish to change our destiny, we need to transform our character, topology and orientation. Assuredly, the road of change toward an ever more mature organization is not easily traveled. Willingness to suffer the uncertain consequences of such a confrontation is indeed rare.

Recall the Chase Manhattan example from Chapter 4. It appears that Chase has the elements in place for a re-vision. Yet, it is only living within the organization that would tell whether they are facing reality or simply creating window dressing. There are many elements that contribute to a successful change effort, and continuous, steadfast attention to those elements as explained in this book is a necessary requisite.

It is a myth that passion for a vision fades. Change is possible with knowledge and requisite courage. Companies succeed because they have the courage to deliver products and services with value superior to alternative competitive values. Very much like this book that offers useful information, it's useless unless it is applied to your organization. It is not the what that is important, but the really important issue is how we deal with the what. Good Luck!

Endnotes

1. For additional perspectives on social transformation see; Drucker, Peter F. (1994) "The Age of Social Transformation," *Atlantic Monthly*, (November); Redfield, James. (1993) *The Celestine Prophecy*, NY: Warner.

2. It is important here to define the term reality, because the existentialists will claim that it is impossible to know reality. On one level, we can concede that true reality might well be outside human comprehension. For example, if everything is relative we might ask the question, "What time does Pittsburgh stop at this train?" Most of us, however, have a more grounded comfort level asking, "What time does this train stop in Pittsburgh?" To do away with this argument of whether reality can be truly known, we will assume that reality is defined to be the world as we know it, with all the information available to us at a specified point in time.

3. Nichols, Martha. (1994) "Does New Age Business Have A Message For Managers?" *Harvard Business Review* (March–April) pp. 52–60.

4. Autry, James A. (1994) *Life and Work: A Manager's Search For Meaning*, NY: Morrow.

5. Covey, Stephen R (1989) *The 7 Habits of Highly Effective People*, NY: Simon & Schuster.

6. Peters, Tom. (1987) *Thriving On Chaos*, NY: Knopf.

INDEX